A WORD IN YOUR EAR

A WORD IN YOUR EAR

How & Why to Read James Joyce's *Finnegans Wake*

by Eric Rosenbloom

∾

Text copyright 2005
Eric Rosenbloom

∾

Pictures and Doodles font copyright 2001
Eric Rosenbloom

∾

Typesetting & design
by
Kirby Mountain Composition & Graphics
Kirby, Vermont
www.kirbymountain.com

∾

current edition
February 2, 2003

∾

ISBN 1-4196-0930
BookSurge Publishing

A WORD IN YOUR EAR

PART I • INTRODUCTION *page 1*

LANGUAGE AND TECHNIQUE	4
Reading Techniques	5
Example of Technique	8
Example of Exegesis	9
CHARACTERS (SIGLA)	12
Relationships	12
Patterns	14
Issy	15
Identity	16
Other Characters	17
Magic Numbers	18
SAINTS GIORDANO AND GIAMBATTISTA	20
Viconian Cycle	22
Death and Rebirth	25
Humanism	26
THE BOOK OF THE DEAD	26
STRUCTURE	29
GEOGRAPHY	29
Dublin	29
The Rest of Ireland	31
HISTORY	32
Prehistoric	32
Christian	34
Norse	35
English	36
Misery	37
Struggle	38
Liberation	40
James Joyce	41
LAST WORD BEFORE READING ON	41

PART II • READING *page 43*

King Roderick O'Conor—pp. 380–382	48
The Kiss—pp. 383–386	50
St. Kevin and the Bath—pp. 604–606	53
Archdruid Berkeley and St. Patrick—pp. 611–612	56
Note on Reading	60
2 FABLES	61
The Mookse and the Gripes (pp. 152–159)	62
The Ondt and the Gracehoper (pp. 414–419)	63
The Fables of La Fontaine	65
ALP	66
HCE	69
13 PASSAGES	
Overture (pp. 3–4)	74
Finnegan's Wake (pp. 4–6)	75
The Book (pp. 18–20)	77
Slander (pp. 33–34)	79
The Ballad of Persse O'Reilly (pp. 44–47)	80
Letter (pp. 104–108)	81
Shem (pp. 169–172)	82
Shem the Penman (pp. 182–186)	83
The Song of the Four (pp. 398–399)	85
Vision of Shaun (pp. 403–405)	85
Farewell to Haun (pp. 471–473)	85
The Letter (pp. 615–619)	86
Anna Liffey (pp. 619–628)	87

APPENDICES *page 89*

A Shorter *Finnegans Wake*	91
The Mystery of the Narrator	92
Cycles of Genesis	93
The Ravisht Bride	96

Ma la fantasia altro non è che risalto di reminiscenze, e l'ingegno altro non è che lavoro d'intorno a cose che si ricordano.
                                                            Giambattista Vico

(But imagination is nothing other than the springing up again of reminiscences, and genius is nothing but working on what is remembered.)

No, it's a wheel, I tell the world. And *it's all* square.
With kindest regards sincerely yours
                                                            James Joyce

Hyl. *But the novelty, Philonous, the novelty! There lies the danger. New notions should always be discountenanced; they unsettle men's minds, and nobody knows where they will end.*
                                                            George Berkeley

PART I
•
INTRODUCTION

Finnegans Wake (1922–1939) by James Joyce (1882–1941), elaborates the fragmentation and reunification of identity during sleep. The masculine (as Joyce characterized it) mind of the day has been overtaken by the feminine night mind. The result is a book that reaches deep into the unconscious soul, beyond language and so before language, but forced to use language to tell it. The characters live in the transformation and flux of a dream, embodying the sleeper's mind.

The human mind, and the history it creates in its image, is protean and complex but not a chaos or void. And so in *Finnegans Wake* certain things stand out again and again as one reads and rereads. What follows is an introduction to some of those patterns and recurring points of order—albeit as seen in my own ever evolving understanding. Knowing some of this as you begin reading yourself will I hope make the book a little less forbidding.

I will not be prescriptive, nor am I trying to prove a thesis. This introduction will avoid obsessive detail and arcana and analysis. The aim is to provide broadly applicable information—along with some of the insights of my experience—from which the reader will certainly venture according to his or her own insights, interests, and character.

Even this general introduction, however, may be a lot to absorb at once. Read it casually before we examine actual passages of the *Wake*. Then come back to it as a reference or foil for your own reading. Page references, unless otherwise noted, are to the corrected edition (8th (1958) printing onward) of *Finnegans Wake* published in the United States by Viking Press.

Language and Technique

The language of *Finnegans Wake* is the first thing you notice. Basically, Joyce has altered words and phrases to reveal or accommodate opposites and correspondences—historical, coincidental, and humorous; *e.g.*, the funeral becomes funferall, and the mighty are mitey. Terms often collide, as in "pentschanjeuchy," combining *pentateuch* and *punch & judy* for an odd new adjective.

He also uses language to emphasize the subject, using Norwegian words, for example, when the Norwegian Captain is the subject, inserting names of rivers in a chapter about the river Liffey, and filling up his version of the fable of the ant and the grasshopper with names of insects and their body parts. Many European and other languages—including "secret" languages of travellers and the underworld (and of priests and scholars)—multiply the layers of meaning and pun.

Sometimes words are altered to fit a metrical or alliterative pattern or to create the sound of accent, dialect, or mishearing,* or just to sound better musically, or to play with variations of a familiar phrase. Occasionally, words are scrambled, or worse. And the hero of the book often stutters: The stammer of a toddler—unsure of his words before his thoughts and senses and figures of authority—becomes the stammer of the authority himself, his hesitancy before the judgement of his peers, history, and his own conscience, struggling still with the ill fit of his few words.

---

*For example, Dublin is sometimes confused with Lublin, Poland, and, as Baile Átha Cliath (*see* Geography, *below*), often identified with Balaclava on the Crimean peninsula, where the earl of Lucan ordered the suicidal charge of the (Irish) light brigade, made famous by Tennyson.

A good example of the way Joyce intertwined and layered meaning is in the name Perce O'Reilly, by which the book's male protagonist, Earwicker, is mocked in a ballad (pp. 44–47). The name comes from the French word for an earwig, *perce-oreille*. It also combines the names of the 2 leaders of the 1916 Easter uprising (*see* History, *below*), Patrick Pearse, a poet who was executed, and "The O'Rahilly," who was killed in the battle. Once Joyce creates a name or word, he then uses that as a basis of other puns, as in "beers o'ryely" (p. 498), which echoes the duality of the character by evoking the scene from the song "Finnegan's Wake": "A gallon of whiskey at his feet, And a barrel of porter at his head."

Imagine an absurdly precocious infant in a family whose every member and acquaintance speaks a different language and sings different songs. Joyce's book is what that child, told to speak English, might say to give form to her Irish soul. As with a toddler's amalgam of language before it has found its conformity, listening to *Finnegans Wake* requires familiarity, concentration, imagination, and patience.

> Now, patience; and remember patience is the great thing, and above all things else we must avoid anything like being or becoming out of patience. [p. 108]

Keep in mind that there are no steadfast rules. There is no key. Or rather there is no single key. Set in Dublin, it is about doubling. The sound of the book is mostly, nonetheless, Irish-accented English. Read out loud: The sound of a sentence is usually more clear than its appearance. The thing to do is take it a bit at a time, as the book progresses in distinctly elaborated units, sometimes by paragraph, sometimes more.

Finnegans Wake is no doubt about it a challenging book, but reading just a few pages is uniquely rewarding. Before long, you will find a great deal of beauty that needs no exegesis.

Reading Techniques

Like Richard Wagner with his operas (bookseller Sylvia Beach thought that *Finnegans Wake* was modeled on Wagner's *Ring*), James Joyce approached his work with a highly developed sense of its mythic importance: "I go to encounter for the millionth time the reality of experience and to forge in the smithy of my soul the uncreated conscience of my race" *(A Portrait of the Artist As a Young Man)*. He wrote the way a violinist loves the bow and strings of his instrument. There is something unnatural about it, and something necessary. His book broadens from personal to national to global memories in a grand affirmation of human identity. Joyce nonetheless recalls what the sentimental refers to—the love and fear that animate our lives—so that all his rigor brings him back to the humane.

Read slowly and listen to the music of the myriad voices. Catch the phrases that recur like motifs: "A pint of porter please!"* "O felix culpa!"† "Up Guards and at 'em!"‡ "Obedientia Civium Urbis Felicitas,"§ "Our exagmination round his factification for incamination of work in progress," ‖ and so on. Notice the lines of song that also contribute to the book's music: from the American vaudeville song "Finnegan's Wake," of course, the *Irish Melodies* of Thomas Moore, "The Wild Man of Borneo," and many many more. Enjoy the word play. And, once in a while, you will come away with a somewhat conscious grasp or a meaningful memory of what you heard in your mind's eye.

For puzzling out specific passages, I recommend first a good (unabridged) dictionary# and then Roland McHugh's *Annotations to Finnegans Wake*, which is a linear compilation of allusions and non-English and uncommon words. An old *Encyclopedia Britannica* is useful, as Joyce owned—and used extensively—the 11th edition. There are books that discuss and index names, songs, places, plants, children's lore, books, opera, sigla *(see below)*, Gaelic,

---

*Also "point of order," the parliamentary motion for a ruling on decorum or procedure, one of the obstructionist techniques used by Charles Stewart Parnell to force the passing of Irish Home Rule.
†From St. Augustine, start of a paschal prayer: *O happy fault, to merit such a redeemer!*
‡Supposed rallying cry at Waterloo from the duke of Wellington.
§Dublin motto: *Citizen's Obedience, Happy City.*
‖ The title of a collection—organized by Joyce and published in 1929—of 12 essays by friends and supporters.
#"He read Skeat's *Etymological Dictionary* by the hour" *(Stephen Hero)*.

Greek, Latin, German, Scandinavian, alchemy, colors, history, sex, riddles, myth, &c., as well as books that more generally look at the book or all of Joyce's work as a whole. Peruse the ones that seem interesting or useful to you. Articles in the *James Joyce Quarterly* and *A Wake Newslitter* (whose archive is available on "compact disc" for computer access) and other regular collections that can be found in a big library can be interesting, as can some of the material now found through the World Wide Web computer network. Participation in a reading group or electronic-mail discussion group can be particularly helpful. Finally, Richard Ellmann's biography is essential, as Joyce's favorite subject—the one he knew the deepest—was himself. By reflecting himself as fully as possible, Joyce has created an astounding mirror for every reader. Brenda Maddox's biography of Nora Barnacle (his wife) is a valuable complement to Ellmann's book.

Keep in mind that the experts may have more experience and specialized knowledge—and anyone can put up a web page—but they have no more insight than any other diligent reader. In fact, many published interpretations are rather a stretch or otherwise dubious. And as critic Marian Robinson has noted—and goes on to prove—explications of *Finnegans Wake* are often more arcane than the text itself. Even the seemingly objective and comprehensive *Annotations* has questionable glosses and huge gaps.

Finnegans Wake embodies Joyce's view of the "chaosmos" (p. 118), our "whome" (p. 296 and elsewhere), and the human understanding of it, namely, *epiphany*. The *Christian* epiphany is the revelation to John—as the first rays of the sun ("Pu Nuseht, lord of risings" (p. 593)) strike the surface of the river—that Jesus was God: "bearing down on me under whitespread wings" (p. 628). We read the veil of appearances and once in a while our senses surge in a vision of what's behind that veil: We feel a momentary harmony with beauty and meaning. And for Joyce, beauty, i.e. artistic, i.e. spiritual, truth, went well beyond the sentimentally pretty or moral to embrace all life, even the low parts. His artistic mission was not to excite desire or loathing but to create arresting moments of joy.

Example of Technique

An example of Joyce's basic technique might be seen in the phrase (which I have made up so that I can confidently discuss its origin), "when bush cons to shrub." This clearly plays on the familiar phrase for decisive moment, "when push comes to shove." By altering the expected words, worlds of meaning are made available; most immediately, the intensification of push to shove is echoed by the concentration of bush (which can refer to a thicket or uncultivated countryside) to shrub, the collective to the specific. Yet at the same time *bush* and *shrub* defy that movement as they are also essentially equivalent terms. *Shrub* even looks like a reflection of *bush*.

If we are compelled to explore further, a dictionary reveals that *bush* once meant *tavern* (for the ivy branch on its signboard or over the door) and that *shrub* is a sweetened citrus drink with rum or brandy: Again, the movement is from the broad to the narrow, and perhaps from the symbolic to the sweetly sentimental. The latter meanings were not part of my original intention, but they are a happy coincidence that I accept—indeed that I must accept if I keep the door open in this way to all possibilities.

The expected *comes* is changed to *cons*, emphasizing the directional movement as an increase in knowledge. It also inserts the ideas of opposition and deceit. And in contemporary American politics, *bush* was the 41st president, George Bush, and *shrub* is what opponents called him and especially his son, also George Bush, who became the 43rd though not quite elected to be. This may suggest a movement from a diminutive to more diminutive, and it adds resonance to the use of *con*.

One might ruminate more on the word *bush* and even relate this example to several themes of *Finnegans Wake*. In fact, with the help of others, I had written several more paragraphs doing so, but this is enough to show the density and richness of meaning (not to mention fun as well as potential tedium) that Joyce's technique makes possible. Note that the technique and the result are not random. First, we see that etymology reveals surprising truths. Not only are things related by their word origins, but unrelated origins often lead to homonymic coincidence. (An example Hugh Kenner gives is Cork (the Irish city, from *curcagh*, swamp) and cork (the bottle stopper, from Arabic-Spanish *alcorque*, itself from Latin *quercus*, oak); Joyce had a picture of Cork, where his father was from, in a cork frame.)

Second, the changes made to the normal written language are deliberate choices. In almost every case more and different changes could have been made but were not (*e.g.*, "whynt pasch caints til shrove," would have taken it in a complex theological direction). And if a change opens doors that confound without adding meaning or sense, it would not be made. Indeed, the language of *Finnegans Wake* is frequently just as it appears—no puns, no double meanings—as in the quote above about patience, and in the first word of the book, *riverrun*.* Keep yourself open to the meanings that suggest themselves as you read, but beware of pretending to see or trying to put in what isn't there.

Example of Exegesis

We will be reading particular passages later but in a broad way—so here is a small illustration of what's involved in a closer reading of a whole passage, building on the techniques of the previous example.

> If Dann's dane, Ann's dirty, if he's plane she's purty, if he's fane, she's flirty, with her auburnt streams, and her coy cajoleries, and her dabblin drolleries, for to rouse his rudderup, or to drench his dreams. If hot Hammurabi, or cowld Clesiastes, could espy her pranklings, they'd burst bounds agin, and renounce their ruings, and denounce their doings, for river and iver, and a night. Amin! [p. 139]

Right away, you notice the strong rhythm, alliteration, and rhyme, how it builds on itself, generating opposites (an important key to reading), counterpointing Ann against Dann and then elaborating the probable reactions of Hammurabi and Clesiastes. We see a male character (Dann the Dane) being matched by a female character (Ann of "dear dirty Dublin," as suggested by the

---
*In which word, nonetheless, one might hear *rêverons*, we will dream.

word *dirty* against *dane*). *Dann* also suggests the early De Danaan people associated with haunted burial mounds in Ireland, so he is both ancient spirit of the land and its Viking invader. Ann, too, is both of the dirt and of the Viking-built city of Dublin.

he's plane she's purty: He's flat—the plain west of Dublin—or a tree as well as the tool that smoothes a tree, and she's pretty (stage-Irish pronunciation) and pert, perhaps in seclusion behind the purdah veil, and the stream purling through the plain.

he's fane, she's flirty: A fane in poetry is a temple, a place for feasting; it is an old word for pennant and weathercock; in Scotland, it is a devil, and it means finished, refined; *flirty* may contain the Galway name *Flaherty* (so *fane* may have the Dublin name *Fagan*). (Joyce was an avid student of old forms and etymology, so I am using the *Oxford English Dictionary*, which he owned as it was published through the 1920s and early '30s.)

Moving on, Ann's auburn tresses become *auburnt streams* as she is the muddy river (and the dreams) the Viking's boat comes up, and she has been oft burnt by earlier invasions, or by a life outdoors. She rouses his rudder (his penis steering for her vagina). And she runs through watering his dreams (*dabblin* suggesting Dublin, dabbling, and doubling, as well as a babbling brook rolling on), and floods his passion or puts his fire out as necessary.

The next sentence pairs two opposed male characters, hot Hammurabi (a law-giving prince) and cold (cowled) Clesiastes (a proverb-giving priest), against a more removed female. It speculates what would happen if they—like the elders of Babylon and Susanna—could see her pranklings. *Prankle* is an old form of *prance*. *Prangle* is a very old word for *squeeze* or *pinch*. And it is about pranks and the Prankquean of pages 21–23, in which the female is counter-invader, and the wrath of her rankling, and perhaps about wrangling and tinkling (spying on her while she urinates).

And there is a code here: HCE is the principal male character, the personification of Dublin, and ALP—the Ann of this passage—is his female counterpart, personifying the Liffey river. Their initials appear throughout the book—in various order—and I will describe these characters in the next section of this introduction. Here, we have *hot Hammurabi–cowld Clesiastes–espy* to denote HCE's presence. The hot–cold personality split corresponds to Ann's firing of and dousing of passion.

Wrapping up, if apart they could espy (suggesting violation) her *pranklings*—what Ann is capable of or the secrets she holds—*they'd burst bounds agin* (break their bonds, overflow their banks, *agin* meaning *again* and *against* each other and rhyming with the *amin* that ends this passage), *and renounce their ruings* (ruins, their past accomplishments, regrets), *and denounce their doings, for river and iver* (forever and ever, for Ann the river, and ivy the symbol of remembrance that came to stand for Charles Stewart Parnell's futile sacrifice for Irish home rule), *and a night* (bringing to mind the thousand nights and a night of the *Arabian Nights' Entertainment*). *Amin!*—meaning *amen*, of course, the affirmative end of a prayer; and, according to McHugh's *Annotations, min* is Dutch for love. In Dutch it also means to nurse. It Hebrew it means sex. Min is an Egyptian fertility—therefore river—god. Amen, for that matter, is a very ancient Egyptian god, whose name refers to the hidden power of conception and who may be invoked throughout the book.

Conclusion. By this example, you can see how stimulating it is to read this book. And how mad you would have to be—or would soon become—if you tried to tease out every thread of allusion or fill out every layer of meaning. On the other hand, such endeavors are richly rewarded, and it is definitely part of the pleasure of *Finnegans Wake.* Some passages in the book demand substantial work before revealing themselves, but as this example shows—I hope not too unfairly—the essence of most passages may be fairly clear in one or two readings without resort to extensive research or elaborate deduction. And even when the meaning is obscure, the music may nonetheless ring clear.

The example also shows what makes reading *Finnegans Wake* possible at all: Its main object of allusion is itself (although that self contains the universe). The book continually reiterates key themes, some of which I will now introduce. (Note: Where the spelling of certain words—namely, Irish ones—is variable, I try to follow Joyce's usage.)

Characters (Sigla)

So many names show up in the *Wake* yet they tend to enact the same drama, going round and round like the book itself: "a long the ... riverrun" (pp. 628–3). Much of the drama was inspired by Joyce's own family and battles: his father John Stanislaus, his earnest brother also named John Stanislaus, his Galway love Nora Barnacle, their schizophrenic daughter Lucia and drifting son Giorgio, his friends and rivals and critics, himself as a skeptic of church and state, the writers he admired and partly identified with (Dante, Shakespeare, Ibsen), his eye problems.

To represent a stock company of players through their changing faces, Joyce in his notebooks used a set of pre-alphabetic (or Cyrillic-like, representing a mix of Greek and Hebrew) characters, called "sigla" by their codifier Roland McHugh They are shown as the Doodles family in a footnote on page 299.

⊓	Pop, HCE
△	Mom, ALP
∧ ⊏	sons, twin-opposites Shaun and Shem —unified as ⋌
⊣	daughter, Issy—and her reflection, ⊢

There are a few others—and earlier versions of some—but these seven (7) are central, the muses that enform the book.

Relationships

When the dreamer's day identity disappears under the dream landscape, ⊓ and △, HCE and ALP, Humphrey Chimpden Earwicker and Anna Livia Plurabelle, city and river, emerge as the prehistoric parents. They are settled in the Dublin suburb of Chapelizod. Their house and pub (public house, the "pint of porter place" (p. 260)) is represented by □, which also stands for the book itself—and the world.

HCE and ALP's younger selves are ⌐ and ⌐, exemplified most prominently by Tristan and Isolde the Fair (Iseult-la-Belle, Isabel), for whose bower Chapelizod is named. (⊓ is then usually cast as King Mark of Cornwall, whose trust Tristan betrays, but he is also Isolde's father, the king of Ireland.) In the medieval romance, Tristan also has a wife back in Brittany (Armorica), Isolde of the White Hands (or Lips), and thus Issy's identity doubles to ⊣⊢. Her siglum is a fallen and broken I.

Shem and Shaun. As well as the age and position rivalries of ⊓ and ⌐, there is a personality split—Tristan as servant and as cad—∧ and ⊏, Shaun the Post and Shem the Penman, angel and devil, saint and sage, submission and doubt, Abel and Cain, Romulus and Remus, patrician and plebeian, imperialist and native, white and black, Esau and Jacob, body and mind, spacial and temporal perception, seeing and hearing, west and east (and *vice versa*, which is the case for many of these divisions), north and south, Norseman and Jew, Christian and Mohammedan, Latin and Greek, yang and yin (yes and no), German and French (the two roots of English), Epicurean and Stoic,* bourgeois and bohemian, fat and thin, sentimentality and lust, have and have-not, *&c.*—woof and warp of the mind's tapestry. They are often called Kevin and Jerry (the latter being the anglicization of the diminutive of Diarmaid). These two are also the rival (twin) banks, represented by stone and tree (by splitting Tristan, *i.e.*, "tree-stone"), of the river Liffey (which is △, so the island at Chapelizod is ⊣⊢ and the bridge across is ⊓—there are in fact 2 pubs in Chapelizod, at each end of the bridge). And they are John Jameson and Arthur Guinness, Dublin distiller and brewer (using Liffey water), and the gallon of whiskey at his feet and the barrel of porter at his head in the song "Finnegan's Wake." Joyce's primary model for Shem was himself as writer, rebel, exile; for Shaun it was what he might have been: clerk, professor, singer, politician, priest.

---

*Giambattista Vico *(see below)* described the Stoics as believing in a deaf chain of cause and effect and a God of infinite mind subject to fate, the Epicureans in a blind concourse of atoms and a God of mere body in a world of chance.

Patterns

1-2-3. One recurring pattern sets ∧ and ⊏—and eventually ⌇, their united front—against ⊓, with ⊣ and ⊢ going between the two sides. The pattern is referred to in almost every antagonistic encounter. The battle of Waterloo, for example, is retold in this way (pp. 8–10: The duke of Wellington is ⊓ against blackmailing Jenny (⊣⊢) and the upstart Napoleon—⊏, ∧, and ⌇ in turn). The children's game of Angels and Devils (pp. 219–259) is a precursor variation in which Izod (⊣) and her friends hide behind Chuff (∧), while Glugg (⊏) fails to guess their colors.

Even more formatively, perhaps, this is the pattern of "the crime in the park" that dogs HCE* (or amalgamates and stands for all that haunts the dreamer) throughout the book, for which the words of ALP (or the dreambook itself) offer hope of redemption.

The Prankquean story (pp. 21–23) shows the pattern in a legend about Grace O'Malley—the Elizabethan-era queen in the west, who controlled the formidable sailing fleet of Galway (a major international port at the time) and organized resistance to the English for decades. She is said to have demanded to see the earl of Howth, who was at his dinner, and kidnapped his son until he would keep his door open to all visitors (or at least to her) during mealtime. Joyce gives it as a courtship, with Δ (acting like ⌇) using ∧ and ⊏ to draw out their father, ⊓. It ends with the earl leaving his house and demanding it be shut. The amusing story of Kersse the Tailor and the Norwegian Captain (pp. 311–332) shows the pattern in a foreign merchant wooing the native daughter. Here, Kersse and the Captain share the characters of both ⊓ and ⌇, although Kersse has the soldiers on his side.

---

*Was he spied urinating, defecating, masturbating?; did he expose himself to a pair of young ladies?; did he spy them urinating or adjusting their clothes?; did he proposition them, and have to contend with their escorts, three Fusiliers?; did he intervene with those 3 men on behalf of those 2 women? in the Hollow, by Wellington's monument, at the Magazine wall?; is he a rebel sought by the English, nervous before a uniform?; an English agent sought by the Fenians?; did he write the "Nausicaa" chapter of *Ulysses*? The crime is vague and adaptive to the evershifting needs of scandal and shame.

How Buckley Shot the Russian General (pp. 339–355) balances the battle of Waterloo with another comical story that Joyce remembered from his father: Irishman Buckley in the Crimean War holds fire (∧) upon seeing the splendid suit and again (⊏) while the Russian defecates, and then (⪽) lets him have it when he wipes himself with a piece of sod ("another insult to Ireland!").

This last situation is referred to throughout the book as a version of "the crime": The father figure exposes his backside while defecating—making himself both vulnerable and offensive—and two young women (or his daughter) and three soldiers (or his sons) get involved in the scandal, scandal that began perhaps with the frank sexual relationship between HCE and ALP that does not seek sanction from church or state. The soldiers and women are derived from the 3 castles on the Dublin (M) shield and the 2 robed women supporting it. In each of the versions of this pattern, references to the others, particularly to the Kersse and Buckley stories, abound.

Her pronunciation round his amanuation for articulation of walk in street. Another pattern—that reflects the writing and reading of the book itself—is that ALP has dictated a letter to Shem for delivery by Shaun to HCE. It is the word of redemption that Finnegan needs to be Finn again. The letter may never arrive—certainly not in its original form or meaning—but knowing it's there at all may be enough. The letter is a leaf of memory.

Issy

⊣⊦ are variously daughters, spies (double agents!), prostitutes, nurses. Throughout the book, they are the young friends of Dublin writer Jonathan Swift: Esther Johnson, the daughter of Swift's employer's housekeeper, whom he might have secretly married, and Hester Vanhomrigh, the Lord Mayor's daughter, who followed him from London (where they met) back to Dublin and died after a crisis between them. He (himself a man of many pseudonyms) called them, respectively, Stella (and Ppt in letters) and Vanessa. (Another Stella is Beatrice Stella Campbell, the popular actress with whom Dubliner George Bernard Shaw enjoyed a lifelong flirtation and occasional outbursts of passion, and for whom he wrote *Pygmalion*.) Issy herself is another Iseult, too: the daughter of Maud Gonne, to whom William Butler Yeats (a reportedly compulsive masturbator—*see* The Book of the Dead, *below*) proposed marriage after failing with her mother.

They are also Alice Liddell and her looking glass dream, the object of Charles Lutwidge Dodgson's, writer Lewis Carroll's, sentimentalizing. (Lewis Carroll is also remembered as a precursor in using spelling tricks and shifting identities in his writing; and he stammered in the presence of adults.)

Wagner was inspired in writing *Tristan und Isolde* by his Zurich affair with his patron's wife: She is both poetic muse and the object of "improper" lust. She is fauna and flora, witnesses to HCE's crime (and victims of his civilization-building), and dove and raven, the Jewish and Norse birds of revelation and messengers of dawn. Issy is the object of, the very spirit of, memory and desire that binds all of the other players.

Identity

It is important to remember that a character usually has more than one identity at a time, because identity changes in relation to each of several other characters. For example, HCE is ⊓ to the dreamer's ⊔ (buried giant, dormant volcano), but as an invader he is ⌐, wooing ⊣ (and they settle down as ⊓ and △); as rival to his united sons (⌐) he is ∧ to their ⊏. Behind these complexities, though, is simple opposition: ∧-⊏ and ⊓-△, or even more simply ⊣-⊢. Meeting face to face with one's opposite-complement (like the writer and the reader at the page of the book) is shown on page 266 as F Ⅎ. "I told you every telling has a taling and that's the he and the she of it" (p. 213).

These "sigla"—like all identity—are not necessarily gender-specific. For example, the two washerwomen in the chapter about Anna Livia are ∧ and ⊏, as are the young women (jinnies) often arrayed against HCE, as well as Biddy (from Brighid) O'Brien and Biddy Doran from the song "Finnegan's Wake." Further, when seen as an aspect of a larger identity, a character often changes roles with or becomes its opposite, but they also move towards each other to unite in a third identity even as each of them achieves his or her own separate unity, which then must double...

The characters metamorphose because their creator's identity is all in flux. The male aspect of that identity is what goes between ⟅ and ⊓ via the flux between ∧ and ⊏, the female what goes between ⊣ and △ mediated by ⊢. The whole self as a point of order goes to ⟅+⊣, then to ⊓+△, and back again. All the children are trying to be the parents, and eventually, everyone does get older and the younger set moves in: ⊣ becomes △; ⊏ becomes ∧ becomes ⟅ becomes ⊓ becomes ⊔⊔. And every character may be all of these at the same time. "It is the same told of all. Many. Miscegenations on miscegenations" (p. 18).

Other Characters

Another pair of characters are S and K, Sackerson and Kate, who work at the pub and are shadows or echos of HCE and ALP (they are like them respectively Norse and native Irish). S first stood for the snake, the native opposed to P, Saint Patrick. S often witnesses (or believes he does) HCE's transgressions, he tells K (or vice versa), and the scandal grows. He also helps the accused to evade the resulting mob.

Numbers of time and space are also given form.

4	provinces, bedposts,* chroniclers, "Mamalujo" (their ass makes 5 [senses]),	✗
7	rainbow colors, days of week (sun, moon, and visible planets), 3 + 4 (east + west), "Floras,"	⊕
12	day and night hours, months, customers, jury, "Murphies,"†	○
28	ovarian days, schoolgirls, "Maggies,"	○
	(Issy and her reflection make 29½ [lunar days])	

---

*Matthew, Mark, Luke, and John,
 Bless the bed that I lie on,
 Two to foot and two to head,
 Four to carry me when I'm dead.
†Or "Morphios" (p. 142) after the son of Hypnos (sleep) that sends human images to the dreamer.

Magic Numbers

Other numbers show up continually. 1132 and 111 are associated respectively, like the phrases using initial letters h. c. e. and a. l. p., with ⊓ and △. Also like them, they often appear in various permutations—as clock times, street addresses, algebraic expressions. I am indebted to correspondent Clarence Sterling for bringing to the knowledge of *Finnegans Wake* readers that, as documented in the "Annals of Loch Cé," in the year 1132, 700 years after the arrival of St. Patrick (in 432, another oft-seen number), Kildare was sacked and the abbess, representing St. Brighid, was raped (*see* History, *below*, and "The Ravisht Bride," in the Appendices). The perpetrator, Diarmaid Mac Murrough, went on to bring about the Norman invasion a few decades later.

Also, according to the "Annals of the Kingdom of Ireland" by the Four Masters,* legendary Irish hero Finn Mac Cool was killed in 283, which is 1132 ÷ 4. (Mac Cool lived near Dublin. His young wife Grania eloped with an earlier Diarmaid, and his son was the poet Oisin, the alleged writer—as Ossian—of James MacPherson's Fingal and Temora poems.) The man who killed him (with a fishing pike) was accompanied by two brothers, and they were all (Æ, E & Λ) slain by a friend of Finn.

In the Biblical book of Genesis, 11:32 is the last verse before the more historical story of Abraham and Sarah begins.

1132 shows the *Finnegans Wake* players: father, mother, 3 soldiers, 2 maidens. Likewise, 111 shows ALP's triple being as a mother goddess. As well, 111 is 1 + 30 + 80, which are the Hebrew numerical values of A, L, and P.

A collection of 111 prophecies is attributed to the Irish St. Malachy (Maelmhaedhoc twisted to the Hebrew for "messenger"). It seems to be a late-16th-century forgery to support the election of a particular cardinal to the papacy. The series of metaphoric pronouncements (in Latin) describe each pope from the time of Malachy to the end of the world, and many of them

---

*Actually 5, like the provinces of Ireland, the fifth represented in *Finnegans Wake* by an ass. The project was led by monk Michael O'Clery and completed on August 10, 1636, the feast day of St. Lawrence.

can be found in Joyce's text. Malachy was named archbishop of Ireland in 1132 (but he was prevented from taking office for 2 years until he *bought* the pastoral staff from his predecessor) and he established there the use of the Roman liturgy (the Irish church, unaffected by the collapse of the Western Roman Empire in the 5th century, had developed quite independently; for example, in honor of the goddess Brighid, baptism was performed with milk). Malachy died in France in 1148, in the arms of St. Bernard, his biographer.

Another number seen a lot is 40, as in the 40 winks of a nap, 40 days and 40 nights of rain, Jules Verne's *Around the World in 40 Days*, 40 weeks of pregnancy, 40 years of wandering. Noah's deluge marks the end of an era, after which the rainbow is the promise of a new dawn. (Noah (⊓) then gets drunk to celebrate and collapses, exposing himself, which his son Ham (⌐) takes advantage of and tells his brothers, Shem (⊏) and Japheth (∧), who cover him up without looking; Ham gets cursed.)

Close to 40 is 39, referring to the Church of England's articles of faith, in which the Irish were forced to be clothed.* 39 Irish MPs joined Parnell (*see* History, *below*) in 1885 to vote with the Tories and force Gladstone's resignation and subsequent negotiations with Parnell to regain the government. And it is 39 days from Christ's birthday to James Joyce's on Candlemas, when the Christian liturgical calendar turns from looking back to the solstitial birth to looking forward to the equinoctial death (*see* "The Ravisht Bride," in the Appendices).

Then there are the thousand nights and a night's entertainment spun by Shahrazade for her sister Dunyazad and which her husband, the sultan Sharyah, listened to—bringing to an end his policy of taking a new wife every night and beheading her in the morning. This number belongs to ALP, because that is the

---

* ' ... that all symbols are properly Clothes; that all Forms whereby 'Spirit manifests itself to sense ... are Clothes; ... and the Thirty-nine 'Articles themselves are articles of wearing-apparel ... ? ' (Thomas Carlyle, *Sartor Resartus*). HCE on page 534: "my dudud dirtynine articles of quoting."

spelling of the first letter in the Hebrew alphabet, *aleph*, which means both one and a thousand.

Issy is often associated with 18, the number of letters in the Irish alphabet, of the Hebrew word for life, *chai*, and of the Moon card in the Tarot, and with 19, the number of years in which lunar and solar calendars resychronize (adopted by Athens in 432 B.C.) and of the college of nuns that kept the sacred fire at Kildare (St. Bride's).

Saints Giordano and Giambattista

Besides characters, there are a few informing spirits behind the work, most notably Giordano Bruno (of Nola) and Giambattista Vico. Giordano was a determinedly independent philosopher burned in Rome by the Inquisition in 1600 after 8 years of imprisonment. He spent his youth—13 years—in the refuge of a Dominican monastery. The 1913 Catholic Encyclopedia characterized his thought as "incoherent materialistic pantheism." From the Copernican solar system he went on to suggest that the sun is not the center of the universe, that creation is infinite, and further that every living thing contains an infinite universe. He said the earth, too, is a living being. Developing the work of Nicholas of Cusa (1401–1464), who said that in God contraries unite, Giordano stated that everything knows itself best in the struggle with its opposite, even creating its opposite for that purpose, or by finding it across time as well as space—or in a mirror—and that no living thing exists except that its opposite exists as well. He envisioned entities in constant flux, exchanging identities, moving farther from and closer to the unity of God. He also worked on a system of memory training, dabbled in alchemy, and believed that Jesus was a magician. He first fled Rome and then many other cities ahead of various church and university authorities, and spent a few very productive years in London as toast of the town. Back in Venice, he was betrayed by his host to the Holy Office. The Nolan's wide-ranging intellect and varied life (much of it in exile) yet singleness of vision represented for Joyce the spiritual unity of character. As such, he is found in Dublin as the stationers Browne and Nolan (who published the edition of Chapman's Homer that Joyce probably read as a child).

Giambattista Vico (1688–1744) was a linguist and legal historian who published his New Science, which he described as "a rational civil theology of divine providence,"* in 1725 and went mad while perfecting it for further editions. Developing many of Giordano's ideas, he too rejected the idea of "golden" ages; the New Science examines the course of nations out of Cyclopean family clearings, divine kings, and the offer of asylum for vassals, through alliance of the "noble" fathers in eternal reaction against the growing demands of the vassals, to a certain equity for all, descent into civil wars and anarchy, and salvation under a civil monarchy. The monarchy (*i.e.*, empire) collapses, and, as divine kings rise again in its wake, barbarism returns and the nations are reborn. The cycle began after the universal flood with a flash of lightning and clap of thunder that drove brutish giants to recall their humanity and hide in shame in caves, there beginning the institutions of religion, marriage, and burial that are at the origin of every civilization. A recourse of the cycle began in Europe after the collapse of Rome.

By examining Greek and Roman history, language, mythology, and law, Vico described the course of nations in terms of the Egyptian ages of gods, of heros, and of people. Each age has a characteristic nature (poetic, heroic, human), reflected in its social organization (family, city, nation), natural law (divine, force, reason), government (theocratic, aristocratic, democratic), customs (religion, social ceremony, civic duty), reason (revelatory, political, personal), language and letters (mute gesture and heiroglyphics, heraldry and symbolism, popular speech and characters), and so on. The heroic age is transitional, transferring the rights and property of Adam to more of the people. It is marked by verbal scrupulousness, punctilious manners, violent struggles, suspicion and

---

*Quotes in the text are from the translation by Thomas Goddard Bergin and Max Harold Fisch, published by the Cornell University Press, Ithaca, New York, copyright 1968 Cornell University Press.

civil turbulence, and *pura et pia bella* (pure and pious war, such as the Crusades that ended the "dark" age of Europe's *ricorso*).

Each age itself goes through a cycle of rising and falling, recovery and demise, ending with a poet—theological, heroic, vulgar—who culminates the age and ushers in the next age by creating a new Jove.

Vico does not limit himself, however, to this 3-stage scheme, describing 5 and 6 stages as well for the unfolding of humanity through necessity, utility, comfort, pleasure, luxury, madness, and "waste of his substance." His scheme can be described as a flux between divine kings defending the special status of the "heros" and a civil emperor protecting human equity. And just as Vico analogizes individual development to speculate about early humanity, Joyce sees a cycle of history in every person's childhood, maturity, and decline.

The major part of the New Science establishes the thought of the divine and early heroic ages, their "poetic wisdom." For example, as a nation's world expanded, local names were re-used for farther places in the same direction. This (along with Dante's finding that he and Florence were a central concern of the divine order in his *Comedy*) provides a model for Joyces' Dublin-based universe ("they went doublin their mumper all the time" (p. 3)). Vico also discovers the true Homer as the collective voice of the Greek peoples, those of the northeast in the *Iliad* and centuries later those of the southwest in the *Odyssey*; this is akin to Joyce's mystery of Finnegan and his incarnation in HCE, Here Comes Everybody.

Viconian Cycle

It is usually said that the four parts of *Finnegans Wake* follow a Viconian cycle of gods–heros–people–recourse. Indeed, "vicus of recirculation" is mentioned in the first sentence, there is a flood followed by thunder later on the first page, and thunder words continue to be heard (pp. 3, 23, 44, 90, 113, 257, 314, 332, 414, and 424*—nine of 100 letters each and one of 101 to total 1001

---

*"The hundredlettered name again, last word of perfect language."

letters). The thunder, however, is like the audible babblings of a fitful sleeper threatening to rise, given form by responses from the players of the book that ensure he will stay down until they are ready, *i.e.*, the book seems to be stuck in the pre-human state of atheist giants, in the Norse Ginnungagap, before (and after) time.

The four parts of *Finnegans Wake* do not follow the Egypto-Viconian ages. If anything, they go backwards, from the rollicking expansiveness of the first book (of the people), through the set-pieces of the second (the heroic family), to the self-worshipping Shaun of the third (the god-like son). Most problematic with the identification of Joyce's parts with Vico's ages is that the recourse (*ricorso* in Italian) is not a 4th age, but the return of the 1st. Instead of following Vico's cycle, the four parts of *Finnegans Wake* may—as Samuel Becket claimed—represent the three institutions (religion, marriage, burial) that move humanity into the light of civilization and, finally, step into history. Kabbalistically, they may represent the archetypal, creative, formative, and material worlds in the process of getting from idea to the manifestation of dawn. They may be simply four different dreams through the deepening night. They may originate from the four parts of the Tristan & Isolde stories.

Joyce, as he does with all his sources, re-interprets Vico to fit his own scheme. He certainly uses Vico, but the heroic age is always in the present, the divine age always in the past, and the popular age in the future; and they are all present simultaneously. Finn Mac Cool with the goddess Brighid is of the divine age, HCE and ALP are of the heroic, and Shem, Shaun, and Issy the popular. Avatars of each of them appear in every age. Cycles spin off from multitudes of events and in myriad lives, overlapping and intertwining and confusing each other. The flood represents the cataclysmic end as well as the pause before going round again.*

---

*The biblical deluge rained down 1,656 years after Creation. 1,656 years after the death of Finn Mac Cool, *Finnegans Wake* was published. For more fun with historical cycles, *see* Cycles of Genesis, in the Appendices.

Nonetheless, *Finnegans Wake* is full of 3- and 4-term sequences; usually they represent the religion, marriage, and burial at the beginning of history, *e.g.*, "Harry me, marry me, bury me, bind me" (p. 408; all 3 institutions are binding: by piety, shame, sense of immortality). Their regularity emphasizes the universality and circularity of human time that Vico stands for in the book. On page 590, the cycle appears very simply as "Tiers, tiers and tiers. Rounds." And on page 452: "The Vico road goes round and round to meet where terms begin." This describes simultaneous opposite movement from a point of unity, joining briefly on the other side and continuing back to the origin.* It describes a flux as much as a cycle, a "systomy dystomy" (p. 597) like the beating of the heart or the fall and rise of all human endeavors.

Joyce, although often referring people to Vico, also asserted he did not "believe" Vico's science, "but my imagination grows when I read Vico as it doesn't when I read Freud or Jung." He was perhaps using Vico to think about the subconscious mind in history more than about history itself. Vico provided the idea that mind and history are identical, and that language betrays their secrets. Thus all history could be revealed in a book of a sleeping soul, its crude projections redeemed in the unconscious mind that created them. (As Stephen Dedalus might have said in his dotage, "History is a nightmare I'm dreaming to wake.")

Hugh Kenner has suggested that the dreamer does not want to wake up, that ALP is a widow resisting the conscious awareness that her husband—executed after the 1916 Easter uprising, he says—is no longer beside her. The hanging scaffold is suppressed by becoming Tim Finnegan's building scaffold. Her tears become the river in which her dreams flow. The book of history assures us that life always rises from the ashes, but we also know that individual loss is unrecoverable. The incomplete sentence at the end of *Finnegans Wake* gives the reader a choice: Leave the book and return to life, or return to the book's first words.

---

*It also refers to Vico's method of tracing words to their common origins.

Joyce once likened *Finnegans Wake* to the *Dark Night of the Soul*, a treatise by shoeless and imprisoned Saint John of the Cross on the perfection of love and his poem *Dark Night*. That work is the fourth part of his *Ascent of Mount Carmel*, and similarly *Finnegans Wake* as a whole is a separate elaboration of Vico's cycle through the nightly unrest of dream. As history courses like the rise, glory, and descent of the sun each day, an individual recourse occurs at night. The language of the book reflects this period of transition from—the flux between—decadence and a new beginning. There is a Vico road in Dalkey, a southern coastal suburb of Dublin.

Death and Rebirth

Joyce once imagined his book as the dead giant Finn Mac Cool lying by the Liffey (where swam the salmon, his totem animal) watching history—his and the world's, the past and the future—flowing through him. This life-in-death dream becomes a sacramental process of rebirth. At Finnegan's wake, Finnegans wake.

One should also remember that Joyce nearly joined the Jesuits, and that the Christian ceremonial cycle continued to shape his imagination. The mystery of the trinity, for example, three persons (multiplicity) representing unity, is very much in the spirit of *Finnegans Wake*. At its best, Christianity has been a great syncretizer and humanizer of older myths. For example, the stations of the cross represent a sacrifice ritual in terms of a human procession, the paschal drama of the rise and fall and rise again of human history. At its worst, it is a great beast devouring, Shaun-like, everything before it in the name of salvation after death.

The Christian sacramental meal, the eucharist, the host, is often present. *Hoc est corpus* ("This is the body") is another manifestation of HCE ("Here Comes Everybody"; but also High Church of England). As host ("victim" in Latin) at his pub, HCE serves and is mocked by his 12 customers. In Vico, the earlier meaning of host is alien, thief, violator of the clearing—an enemy of the people who is sacrificed in their name. The first cities were identified with the altars that were in the fields, where, for example, Cain slew the more primitive Abel and Romulus slew Remus who jumped over the just-plowed boundaries. It is alienated Hosty who writes "The Ballad of Persse O'Reilly" (pp. 44–47) against the outsider HCE.

Vico called the course of nations a history of piety, and in their recourse they were guided by Christianity, a more human religion. For Joyce, Christianity is more prominent than other religious and mythological systems because it is the one he knew intimately. But the eucharistic meal—the renewing sacrifice—fits the pattern described in James George Frazer's *The Golden Bough** of killing and eating a divine king. And it is connected with the Jewish feast of tabernacles, or Succoth, as a turning of the year. Although it is now only theater, the original barbaric act ("He'll want all his fury gutmurdherers to redress him." (p. 617)) still erupts into history and continues to reverberate in the human unconscious.

Humanism

My use of the term is not philosophically rigorous, but Vico and Giordano are important also as humanists. Giordano's love of God was such that he loved nature as it is. He showed that the infinitude of the divine is within every element and creature of nature and every human being. Vico showed that history was not a matter of destiny or fate, but the operation of divine providence in the human mind; he insisted that "the world of civil society has certainly been made by men, and that its principles are therefore to be found within the modifications of our own human mind."

THE BOOK OF THE DEAD

Another model of cyclical rebirth that Joyce draws from is the Egyptian *Book of the Dead*, or *The Chapters of Coming-Forth-by-Day*. According to legend, the Irish language was brought by Fenius (a Phoenician) and Druidism was akin to Egyptian religion.

---

*Frazer showed that the golden bough, used by Aeneas to enter the underworld, was mistletoe. Vico showed that is a stalk of grain.

The Book of the Dead is a guide to the many-portaled labyrinthine otherworld—Amenta—and its myriad denizens. It includes incantations for the recently deceased and bound (as mummies) to make their way towards joining Osiris (his court is in the marshes of Sekhet Hetep) in the boat of the sun on its nightly journey under the earth† to rise as the day. Osiris (⊓) is also the corn (or the golden bough), buried in the Nile mud to rise again to be cut down and eaten (and brewed) and some of it saved to be buried again for a new cycle.

The story involves his mother-sister-wife Isis (△) gathering up his pieces (re-membering him) after their brother-son Set (⊏) has torn him apart and scattered them. Isis's tears cause the Nile to rise. She makes a clay phallus to replace the penis she can't find. Her copulation with him frees (creates) their other son Horus (∧) to battle Set and retrieve the eye that he kept. Horus rises with Isis as the new sun, and Osiris is left to copulate with his mother-sister-daughter Nephthys (⊣). Set kills him again, and Horus is swallowed up by Hathor, the body of night and flood.

Osiris is present in the day in the 3 aspects, ∧, ⌅, and ⊏. They are the rising sun that has supplanted him, the mid-day sun that outshines him, and the setting sun that marks his demise and promise of return. Osiris in the night is ⊔, the dreamer of *Finnegans Wake*. In his journey towards rebirth, it is Isis who puts him together again, recalling, even remaking, his youth. The day world belongs to Horus, the night to Set.

It is as ⌅, at the peak of his power, that Osiris as the unity of ∧ and ⊏ violates their sister and mother in the person of Nephthys, his daughter, an act that echos Joyce's "crime in the park." This begins his descent, until his destruction by Set, which is also the victory of Set over Horus. Then follows the night journey to dawn and the rejuvenation of Osiris in Horus.

---

†The four "children of Horus" (pillars of the sky) guard Osiris in the underworld—two at his feet, two at his arms—like Mamalujo at the four corners of the sleeper's bed. Also like Mamalujo, three of them have animal heads and one a human. An older Egyptian conception of the sky is that it is a woman's torso, the four pillars her arms and legs: At night she swallows the sun and gives birth to it anew each morning.

More than any other source or precursor, this sun-cycle is helpful for approaching a conceptual framework for *Finnegans Wake*. The story, in all its fragmented remembrance—and complicated syncretism—is echoed in much of what haunts Joyce's dreamer. Above all, the characters of the drama correspond very closely to Joyce's, even in their shifting into and out of each other, in △ running through it all, and in ⊔⊔ containing them all.

The guide through this world of the dead is Thoth, the messenger of the gods and inventor of the alphabet. He is also the master of the mysteries of city and house building, because the alphabet provides the bricks of the civilized mind.

Osiris is sometimes identified with his father, Atem (or Tum or Tim &c.),* who created the people of the world by masturbating onto a mudheap at Anu† (Heliopolis). As defecator and masturbator in the park, HCE similarly parodies the regeneration of the mud from the Nile's flood. The pun with *Adam*, the first man, is obvious. After eating the fruit of paradise, when God took his afternoon stroll Adam was behind a bush—very likely defecating after his meal: "the muddest thick that was every heard dump" (p. 296). Atem also established laws and principles of justice, just as HCE is a city builder. Whether in domestic or in mythologic circles, Joyce assumed that sin and creation are the same thing, and James Atherton suggests that Joyce likened Atem's creative act to Ibsen's symbol of spilled tea upsetting sterile social intercourse.‡

**Atem* concidentally in German means breath or spirit.
†Anu is also the name of a Babylonian sky god. The "Paps" in southwest Ireland are named for the great pre-Celtic goddess, also called Anu, Danu, or Anna (the Morrigan is her death aspect; the swan and the salmon are her river aspects).
‡Every city has its presiding goddess, or *thea*. Tara *(Teamhair) (see* Geography, *below)* is named for Tea, the wife of Heremon *(see* History, *below)*. The letter that will redeem HCE's efforts is stained by spilled tea, the color of the Liffey.

Structure

Beyond the Viconian recourse and Osiris at night, the narrative movement of *Finnegans Wake* is towards unity. Chapters 3 & 4 and 6 & 7 could easily be combined, but instead the first section of the book has 8 chapters of roughly equal length. For Joyce, 8 was a number of completeness, and it was a feminine—and a night—number, as with the 8 parts (in 2 sentences) of Molly's chapter that ends *Ulysses*. Reclining, it is the symbol of infinity, ∞. After the opening section of 8 chapters, the book splits into 2 sections of 4 chapters each, then ends with a 1-chapter section, itself made up of 8 parts followed by the farewell soliloquy (pp. 619–628). (The 8 parts begin on pp. 593, 597, 599, 601, 601, 606, 609, and 612. The first 5 of these also make up a single section in which the questions why, how, where, who, and what are answered.) The book begins with the 8-letter word, *riverrun*.

Part I, after describing the fall (into sleep), introduces the fallen hero's stand-in, HCE, and describes the dramas and players that come with him. Part II focuses on the Earwickers as a family, ending with the union of Tristan and Isolde on a departing ship, leaving the elders behind with their memories. Part III follows Shaun's effort to carry a letter for ⊓ and become the sun as dawn approaches. Part IV describes the river Liffey slipping out to sea (the dream dissolving back into the unconscious) before the city of Dublin wakes.

Geography

The body of the sleeper becomes the landscape of memory as he or she expands to fill history and the world, time and space. A familiarity with the geography and history that shape *Finnegans Wake* is therefore essential. Following are some of the basics.

Dublin

Names. Dublin is from Dubh Linn (Dyfflin to the Danes), for "Black Pool," where the Poddle river joins the Liffey from the south. (The

Poddle arises from the same mountain as the Liffey *(see below)*, and in Dublin it has been underground since the end of the 18th century.) (The Tolka river runs through north Dublin.) The "dark pool" was where the Vikings kept their ships and built a city. The overlooking ridge was called Drom Cuill-Choille, or "Brow of a Hazelwood." There was already a small settlement upriver a bit called Baile Átha Cliath (pronounced Bla-cliu or Balaclia or Ballyclee), meaning "Town of the Ford of the Hurdles," *i.e.*, of the wickerwork causeway (each hurdle called a kish, also the name for a wicker basket). Earlier, it was the capital city of the Blani tribe and called Eblana, although this may have been imagined from a corruption of *Dubh Linn*. A name in *Finnegans Wake* that is associated with Dublin is Adam Findlater, a prosperous 19th-century grocer who devoted his money to civic restoration, including a church (Protestant).

Phoenix Park is a large walled preserve west of Dublin and across the river from Chapelizod. The residence (in turn) of viceroy, chief secretary, governor-general ("Uncle Tim's Cabin," "Healiopolis"—*see* History, *below*), and president is there. In *Finnegans Wake*, the park, particularly at the wall of the Magazine Fort, is the site of the "crime" and therefore of many encounters; it is Eden, where the fall into knowledge is enacted nightly; it is the site of Humpty Dumpty's wall and Tim Finnegan's scaffold. The name is a corruption of *fionn-uisge*, meaning clear water. (*Usquebaugh*, meaning water of life, is the source of "whiskey.")

Howth Head extends into the sea to form, with the isthmus of Sutton, the northern boundary of Dublin Bay. Howth is the head of the sleeping giant under the city (his toes are in Phoenix Park). The first earl of Howth was Armory (*i.e.*, of Brittany) Tristram, who defeated the Danes there on August 10, 1177. As this was St. Lawrence's day the earl adopted that name for his family.

Anna Liffey divides Dublin into north and south halves. The name is probably from the Irish "eanach life," meaning *leafy fen*, for the marshes of its estuary; or perhaps from "Abna na Lifé" (p. 496), meaning *brown river*. It has been walled in to allow building on the delta over which it would naturally flood. The Liffey's origin in the Wicklow mountains south of Dublin is only a dozen miles from the mouth. It makes a great (drooping) clockwise loop, whose circuit is renewed by evaporation and rain. Beyond Chapelizod, farther up the river, lie Lucan and, marking the extent of the salmon's run and the edge of the Vikings' domain, Leixlip.

The Rest of Ireland

Ulster (with its main city Belfast) is in the north, Munster (Cork) in the south, Leinster (Dublin) in the east, and Connacht (Galway) in the west. Tara—in the royal precinct of Meath northwest of Dublin overlooking the river Boyne—was the seat of the high king *(ard ri)*. The Pale was the region of strict English control around Dublin.

Names. Much of this information is in Louis Mink's *A Finnegans Wake Gazetteer*. In Irish, the name of the island is Eire. The Tuatha De Danaan *(see* History, *below)* rotated rule among 3 kings, and the name of the island among 3 queens: Eire, Banba, and Fodhla (it was Eire when the Miletians—*see* History, *below*—invaded). Erin is from the Irish for "west island." It was known by the Greeks as Ierene. The Latin name is Hibernia, imagined to be from the Iverni tribe and related to Iberia, but more likely derived from the Greek. Scotia was the name common in the middle ages, from the iron-age Miletians' claim to be from Scythia. (Scotland's name is from the same Irish Scotti who invaded and settled there.) "Ireland" is what the Vikings called it. In France, where Joyce wrote *Finnegans Wake*, one would hear the island's name as "ear-land" (so the Liffey is Ireland's ear-canal into which Earwigger (HCE, "Eirewaker") crawls).

Erse, for "Irish," is from the Norwegian; Irsk is Danish. Gaelic refers to the Q-Celtic tongue that includes Irish, Scottish, and Manx. It take its name from the Gaelli tribe of northeast Ireland, who also settled in Scotland. (Welsh, Cornish, and Breton are the vestiges of the later P-Celtic, or Brittonic, language.)

Ireland is personified as Cathleen ni Houlihan, Shan Van Vocht (Poor Old Woman), and Grace (Grania) O'Malley. There are also endless images from poetry and song, such as James

Clarence Mangan's "Dark Rosaleen." Joyce identifies her in Brighid, also known as Bridget, Bride, and, in Wales, ffraid.

History

Irish history is often seen as a series of invasions, each invasion serving to unite the previous colonizers with their subjects—united Irish all against the common enemy, briefly ending one set of battles to regroup for a new one. Thus the Fir Bolg invaded to rule the Fomorians; they both fought the Miletians, who joined them in subjection to Christianity, and they were all raided by the Vikings; everybody found common cause against the Normans, and with them in turn against Protestant rule, eventually throwing off the yoke of the empire enough to pursue their own wars.

There may be a Viconian set of eras divided by the years 432 (when St. Patrick, ⌇, arrived and won over the sod, ⊔⊔) and 1132 (when the Irish church became completely a part of the Roman city, ⊓⊓). Then 1832 (marking another 700-year period) would have begun a *ricorso*, a return to the primitive state. In fact Catholic emancipation under Anglican rule had just been attained but now a continuing series of martial emergencies began—threatening the progress of democracy and the broader access to shopping that HCE is often concerned with.

Please be reminded that all historiography is politically colored, and Ireland's even more so; I have weighed several sources, ancient and modern, to attempt here a fair account of the highlights relevant to reading *Finnegans Wake*.

Prehistoric

Parthalonians, Nemedians, and Fomorian sea raiders are legendary first settlers, probably of the neolithic age. Their megalithic dolmens and passage graves are still seen. Earlier mesolithic colonists are known by their midden heaps left on the shores of the sea and lakes. The Partholonians lived in the Dublin area (the Liffey plain) and were decimated by plague. Partholon is credited with inventing the alphabet. They are buried at Tallacht (from *thaimhleacht*, plague-grave, which has anglicized to *hamlet*). The Nemedians fled the island after being routed in battle by the Fomorians. The early bronze age was brought by the Fir Bolg who came to rule the whole island. Their gods were preserved in Christian histories as the Tuatha De Danaan (people of the god whose mother is Danu, or Anna), who were said to have conquered the Fir Bolg and much later became the wee people of the fairy mounds. Fomorians continued to raid from the sea. The Celtic Miletians invaded 200 years later (from Spain), dividing their iron-age rule between the brothers Heremon and Heber until Heremon (the north) killed Heber in battle. The ousted Fir Bolg rebelled with the Fomorians 200 years later and after 100 years regained the kingship, to lose it 60 years later.

In the 2nd century A.D. Owen More wrested the southern part of Ireland from high king Conn of the Hundred Battles. The border had been marked by the Esker Riada, a road from Dublin bay to Galway bay. The north-south division continued in later centuries, and the legendary high kingship of Tara was generally a self-delusion except when—most notably by Brian Boru *(see below)*—it was imposed by force on the other provinces.

The Ollave (or *ollamh*) in these times was a master poet who rivalled his king in power. He was an expert in law and conferred with his fellow ollaves by the secret Ogham sign language derived from the Greek alphabet. He was dangerous because of the power of his satires. To wear the 6-colored mantle of chief poet, the ollave had to master 150 Ogham ciphers, 350 long histories and romances (with incidental poetry and harp accompaniment), more poems, philosophy, law, etymology, music, augury, medicine, astronomy, rhetoric, foreign languages, and extemporaneous poetry in 50 different meters.

Did Joyce set out in *Finnegans Wake* to meet these standards? Some critics say he did. What is certain is that Joyce took the language of the occupier, which, like all language in which we must express our deepest experiences, was imposed on his soul like an ill-fitting suit, and he determined to rework what was given him that it might flash with the fabled magic of the Celtic bards.

Christian

Around 403, legends say, a young man named Sucat and his sisters were kidnapped in Roman Wales and enslaved in northwest Ulster (probably Donegal). He escaped after 6 years, apparently prostituting himself to pay for ship passage. Back home, tortured by his sins, he dreamed of a man named Victoricus carrying countless letters; one was given to him, and on seeing the first words, "The voice of the Irish," he heard their voice crying by the wood of Foclut to ask him to walk among them once more. ("Foclut" is usually thought to be from the Irish for "wolf," *i.e.*, *faolchú*, but probably refers to the Fochla kingdom of tribes.) He pursued religious study and got the name Patricus*—from *pater civium*. He returned to Ireland (from France) in 432 to light a Paschal fire on the Hill of Slane opposite King Leary's Beltane (May Day) festival at Tara. He held his own against Leary's druids in a contest of wit, and Leary granted him protection. His generosity with money and gifts helped him prevail over other adversaries. Ireland (but not Leary) converted without a fight—in fact many Irish were already Christian (Patrick was the 2nd bishop sent to them)—and Celtic laws and customs were generally preserved. Besides revealing the native shamrock as a symbol of the Christian Trinity and ridding the island of snakes, Patrick is credited with introducing whiskey (later, HCE brings porter back). Patrick's sister Lupita had become a prostitute and was pregnant when they met again. He ran her over with his chariot until she was dead.

St. Bridget was a friend (and rival) of Patrick and is identified with the goddess of fire and fertility, poetry and milk,† Brighid (pronounced between *bride* and *breed* and *brood* with a breath in the middle). She founded Kildare ("church of the oak") in Magh Life ("plain of the Liffey") in her father's kingdom. It became a great school of the arts. In later years, in the face of Viking raids,

---
*Patricius is the name also of St. Augustine of Hippo's father (his mother's name is Monica (which is Italian slang for a nun)); Augustine is James Joyce's middle name.
†And ale, as Patrick is patron of whiskey.

her relics were moved to be interred with Patrick and Colum *(see below)* at Downpatrick. Bridget's feast day is the 1st of February, her year beginning the next day, James Joyce's birthday. This was also the old Celtic new year. With Patrick's arrival, the year began with the solar equinox, after *his* feast day.

In the 6th century, the master poet Colum (later Saint Columba and called Colum Cille, "Dove of the Church") established several monastic centers for manuscript illumination, most notably Iona (then called simply "I" or "Y"), to which—according to the usual story—he fled after a judgement against him by high king Diarmaid for a copy he made of a psalter ("To every cow her calf"). The other story is that he was forced into exile for instigating war either to recover his book or against Diarmaid to avenge the slaying of a cleric under his protection. Iona vied with Patrick's Armagh for primacy in the Irish church (Scotland was an Irish province). In 575 Colum negotiated autonomy for the Scots, and in 585 he negotiated the survival of the bardic order against resentful princes.

Around 800, Iona produced a highly decorated (and unfinished) gospel. When the community fled the Vikings, it was taken to the monastery at Kells (northwest of Dublin, founded by a successor of Columba), although Kells was repeatedly sacked as well. The book may actually, however, have been produced at Kildare around 900. In 1006 it was stolen, to be found buried 20 days and 2 months later, the gold gone from its case. Joyce always kept close at hand—through his many moves—a volume of commentary and reproductions of this masterpiece. On page 122 of *Finnegans Wake*, the "Tunc crucifixerant" page of the Book of Kells is said to have been inspired by the tea-stained sheet of letter paper scratched out by a hen (named Biddy, an incarnation of Brighid) in the midden heap. As under the Druids, so it was under the monks: an island famous for scholars and ornamental craft.

Norse
Vikings (Finn-Galls and Dubh-Galls, fair and dark foreigners, Norwegians and Danes) began raiding in 793 to plunder the

monasteries. The Norwegian Olaf established Dublin as a trading and raiding base in 837, settling south of the Liffey. After the English arrived they lived primarily on the north side, called Oxmanstown from *ostman*, a Viking trader. (Olaf, meaning ancestor, is the source of the name Humphrey (as well as Hamlet and Havelock) through English corruption of the Irish spelling, Amhlaoidbh.) The modern names of the 3 eastern provinces come from the Vikings: Ulaids-tír, Laigins-tír, and Mumans-tír (there were 4 others besides these at the time).

The battle of Clontarf in the northern suburbs of Dublin was in 1014 between high king Brian Boru and Sitric Silkenbeard, the king of Dublin. It is commonly described as the driving out of the Vikings, the Irish having mastered the invader's weapons and slaughtering them in their retreat through the streets of Dublin. But it was also the culmination of Brian's harassment of the king of Leinster. And many Vikings joined Brian against their rivals. Both sides lost heavily, and nothing changed concerning the Vikings' rule of Dublin. The fight was on Good Friday, so instead of fighting Brian stayed in a nearby wood to pray. He was killed anyway when fleeing Danes came across his tent.

English

In 1166, Roderick (or Rory) O'Conor of Connacht became high king after killing the king from Ulster. The despotic king of Leinster (Diarmaid Mac Murrough or Murchada) was driven out, with the help of Vikings and O'Conor, by the man whose wife he had stolen away some years earlier (fathering Eva (Aoife) with her before she was recaptured and founded a church). Diarmaid found Henry II in France and eventually enlisted the earl of Pembroke (Richard fitz Gilbert de Clare, or Strongbow) with the promise of the Leinster kingship and Eva. Other Normans, Flemings, and Welsh then joined him. (The Joyce name came with the Welsh Normans. The Normans themselves descended from Norsemen who settled in France.)

In the face of this threat, Roderick restored Leinster to Diarmaid, but in 1169 Strongbow came anyway (to Waterford), married Eva, and, led by Diarmaid through the Leinster forest, took Dublin upon the surrender of Archbishop Lawrence O'Toole (Diarmaid's brother-in-law) after the Norwegian king's flight. They were besieged by O'Conor but slipped out for a successful attack; O'Conor, bathing in the Liffey, barely escaped. King Henry arrived in 1172 to keep Strongbow in his place. Taking Ireland for the Pope also absolved Henry of the recent murder of Archbishop Thomas à Becket—"larrons o'toolers clittering up and tombles a'buckets clottering down" (p. 5). Eventually, King Roderick's daughter married the newly installed viceroy and Roderick returned to his Connacht kingship, to be embattled by his sons and finally deposed in 1190 by a nephew. He retired to Cong Abbey.

Misery

Centuries followed of war, pestilence, famine, segregation, rebellion, and repression, including slavery in the West Indies and culminating in the Penal Laws against language, clothing, music, religion, &c. Religious differences had further aggravated things when England broke with the Roman church. Henry VIII and his successors persisted in campaigns of violence and confiscation to fill Ulster's fine farmland with Scottish Presbyterians. Oliver Cromwell paid a murderous visit in 1649 in revenge for the 1641 rebellion of the Catholic earls. A few years later, he banished the whole population "to Connacht or Hell" and established Protestants as the landowners in Leinster and Munster. The Travellers, Ireland's "gipsies," probably originate from this period of eviction.

The battle of the Boyne (north of Dublin) was fought in 1690 between the recently installed Dutch-supported Protestant king, William (III) of Orange (who was his rival's nephew and son-in-law), and the French-supported just-deposed Roman Catholic, James II. The viceroy at the time, the earl of Tyrconnell, and the leader of his army, the earl of Lucan, were loyal to James, and they consolidated Irish support. They lost—not decisively, though, until a year later—and the penal laws soon began. The Irish-mocking song "Lilliburlero" was written during this time.

Uprisings came more frequently. Inspired by the American and French revolutions, Theobald Wolfe Tone, a Protestant, united Catholics and the Ulster Presbyterians against the English empire. He secured French help: Their first expedition in 1796 failed owing to storms, and the second, to help the general uprising of 1798, was intercepted. Wolfe Tone killed himself before he was executed. Union with Great Britain followed as a solution to "the Irish question."

Robert Emmet was executed for attempting another insurrection in 1803. Various insurrectionist "Fenian" groups (*e.g.*, White Boys, United Irishmen, Men of '98, Invincibles) continued to fight for an independent republic. (The word "Fenian" comes from *Fianna*, the king's guard that Finn Mac Cool was chief of.) The Young Ireland organization staged a futile uprising in 1848. The Irish Republican Brotherhood of Ireland and the U.S.A.—formed in 1858 out of the ashes of Young Ireland—organized a rebellion in 1867, led by James Stephens. Despite the military expertise of American veterans of the civil war, they were defeated and most of the leaders imprisoned.

The potato blight of 1845–1848 had further displaced and decimated the population by eviction and famine and disease and emigration (usually to America, including Boston, Mass., although many got only as far as Liverpool). Robert Peel responded effectively, which caused his loss of the government, and the liberals took a disastrous *laissez-faire* approach.

Struggle

Daniel O'Connell ("The Liberator") founded the Catholic Association in 1823, organizing the whole of Catholic Ireland to vote (they had been given the right in 1793) for the cause of emancipation. This brought an end to the penal laws in 1829 (in a bill introduced by the prime minister, the duke of Wellington). In 1841, O'Connell began agitation for the repeal of Union. In 1870, Isaac Butt (a Protestant, and a Unionist until the famine) began the Home Rule party. Charles Stewart Parnell, called "The Chief," was a Protestant landlord from Wicklow who was also president of Michael Davitt's progressive and enormously successful Land League, unifying the two major strands of Irish unrest. After Butt's death in 1879, Parnell was able to lead the Irish votes in parliament in a strategy of obstruction until they got their way. William Gladstone was prime minister.

Parnell had a nervous, cold, and detached manner and was ruthless, superstitious, somnambulistic, subject to severe depression, and a poor public speaker—and he spoke with a Cambridge accent. Joyce claimed he stuttered. He rallied popular support behind his nonviolent cause and was called by Tim Healy "The Uncrowned King of Ireland." Joyce called him the Irish Moses. His mother was born in America.

Momentum for home rule was strong—especially after the Land League was suppressed and its leadership arrested in 1881 and soon released when Gladstone realized things were only worse without them. In 1882, the new chief secretary and his undersecretary were hacked to death in Phoenix Park by the Invincibles, a group formed out of the Fenians earlier absorbed into the Land League, but even this outrage was quickly overcome. Gladstone introduced a home rule bill in 1885 but was defeated, losing the government the next year.

Parnell's involvement in the Phoenix Park murders and other crimes was charged in 1889 in a series of articles, including a reproduced letter, by the London *Times*. At a hearing, it was noticed that the source, Dublin journalist Richard Pigott, in another letter (of blackmail) spelled "hesitancy" as "hesitency," as it also appeared in the letter claimed to be written by Parnell. He confessed to forgery, fled, was pursued, and shot himself dead in Madrid. Support in England for Parnell was again strong.

But later in 1890 Parnell was named in the divorce of his colleague "Captain" William O'Shea from his wife, Kitty, raising the bishops against the Protestant they never liked anyway. (O'Shea in 1881 had challenged Parnell to a duel, but his wife pacified him.) English allies rejected him, and parts of his own party split away, led by Parnell's protegé, Tim Healy. Others in the coalition—the Fenians, the Gaelic revivalists, the socialists (both agrarian and urban)—also split off. Parnell died in Brighton the next year (on October 6, henceforward known as Ivy Day), a few months after marrying Kitty, and nine-year-old James Joyce wrote a poem, "Et tu, Healy."

Parnell is supposed to have challenged his erstwhile colleagues, "When you sell, get my price," and when he went from county to county like a hunted deer he begged the people not to throw him as a sop to the English wolves howling around them. As Joyce wrote in 1912 (in a Trieste newspaper article), "It redounds to their honour that they did not fail this appeal. They did not throw him to the English wolves; they tore him to pieces themselves."

When Gladstone returned to power in 1892 and passed a home rule bill the next year, it was rejected by the Lords.

Liberation

In 1900, Arthur Griffith, editor of the *United Irishman* weekly newspaper, founded the Sinn Féin ("Ourselves Alone") party for independence. He modelled his efforts after the successful liberation of Hungary from Austria. By 1912, home rule might have been achieved, but forces in Ulster took up arms against it. And against them forces in Dublin took up arms. Further debate was then postponed for the war in Europe. In 1918, in response to England's enthusiastic executions and imposition of martial law after the 1916 Easter uprising, Sinn Féin swept elections and established their own assembly, *dáil éireann*. A war for independence followed, fought mainly against the Black and Tans, an English police force specially recruited from recent war veterans.

To thwart Sinn Féin, England granted home rule in 1920, establishing 6 counties of Ulster as a separate dominion. Sinn Féin negotiated a treaty in 1921 establishing an Irish Free State within the Commonwealth. Tim Healy was the first governor-general. Civil war ensued. Eamonn de Valera, American-born in 1882 with a Spanish father, resigned as Griffith's vice president to lead the nationalists. Michael Collins, hero of the war for independence, led the treaty supporters. Griffith died suddenly in 1922, and Collins—now president—was killed 10 days later in an ambush. De Valera gave up armed resistance in 1923 to work politically for greater independence. His party, *Fianna Fáil*, gained power in 1932 and passed a new constitution in 1937 that all but established the republic of today. Enthusiastic censorship of the arts was one unfortunate program of the new government.

James Joyce

After he got his bachelor's degree, Joyce went to Paris to write and think and be hungry for a few months. In 1903, he returned to Dublin as his mother was dying. He met Nora Barnacle, who was working at Finn's Hotel. He wrote to her, "Is there one who understands me?" They left together in 1904 for Pola, Italy, and a job for him at the Berlitz language school. The job never materialized, and after a couple years there and a few months in Rome, they settled in Trieste. After spending the great war in Zurich, they moved to Paris in 1920. They legitimized their marriage for the state there in 1931. James Joyce died in Zurich while the 2nd great war raged around him. His published works (besides articles and reviews) before *Finnegans Wake* include *Chamber Music*, poems; *Dubliners*, short stories; *A Portrait of the Artist As a Young Man*; *Exiles*, a play; *Ulysses*; *Pomes Penyeach*; and most parts of *Finnegans Wake* under the title "Work in Progress."

LAST WORD BEFORE READING ON

Now this is an awful lot of material to absorb in such an abrupt manner without any context. But it is relevant, as everything mentioned is an important part of the book. Again, *Finnegans Wake* is not random or surreal. Its language suggests the pre-conscious roar of the unconscious mind—or a post-conscious babble—yet it is based on observed patterns of history and myth as evidence of the informing human mind or soul. Remember the metempsychosis of *Ulysses*: "That means the transmigration of souls." In *Finnegans Wake*:

> Yet is no body present here which was not there before. Only is order othered. [p. 605]

It is obvious to say that this book is not a normal narrative. But it is important to remember when you read it. The book is like a crystal, and you can burrow in at any point, and from differnt points at different times: Gradually, patterns of reflection and echo, and then the music, begins to be seen.

PART II
•
READING

In *Finnegans Wake* every part contains the whole, so it's possible to get a sense of this roaring ocean of words with a dip of the toe, so to speak, and occasionally wetting both feet to the ankles. I will excerpt and walk you through four short passages that came from the first sketches Joyce wrote (in 1923) after a year of assessing everything he had written before. Then I'll introduce two fables (and provide some guidance through them) and then two longer sections about ALP and HCE. After these, I'll point you towards several other short passages. You may also want to look at the passages already mentioned in the introduction.

When first reading a section, don't worry about understanding it. Especially when the passage is obscure, see if one sentence or phrase makes any sense to you right away. From that kernel, and perhaps considering any detectable clues of the language itself, you may start to get an idea of the section's meaning. Reading on may help to illuminate what has preceded. Sometimes a helpful hint, or even a clear explanation, is found hundreds of pages away, so don't get too hung up in one place.

Remember that plot is rarely the point. As in music, Joyce's primary technique is to create a resonance, such as the evocation of war in the book's fourth paragraph and the melancholy beauty of passing time remembered in the book's last pages. Also like music, much of the meaning of *Finnegans Wake* is in the sound and rhythm of its words.

Having picked up a few clues, re-read the section. Slowly. If an excess of detail or digression is confusing things for you, try to skip through it to stay with the main threads (this is what I will do with the four sketches that follow). Then repeat the process as desired, taking in more each time. Don't worry about moving on if your sense remains vague. Even to experienced readers who can claim a fair enjoyment of the book, many details remain murky while actually reading. One can probably conclude that this was Joyce's intent. Close analytical reading of particular passages may illuminate some of the intense complexity underlying the work, but the work as a whole remains, shimmering and elusive, well outside that analysis.

Joyce likened his book to medieval Irish book illumination, which intertwined the text with animal, human, vegetal, and abstract forms in layers of intricate knotwork, the point being not to follow every strand but to let your senses dance about in its complex design. As with opera, which Joyce also loved, you should not be trying to stay on top of every detail of the story or grasp every word that is sung (often in a language other than your own), but rather enjoying the beauty and emotional power of the song.

Joyce was also following the ancient tradition among Celtic bards of wordplay and cipher, inspired by the variability and generosity of the Irish tongue itself. The non-speaker can see it in the spelling, where Kevin is *Caoimhghen* (cave-hen), Finn Mac Cool is *Fionn Mac Cuimhaill*, and, as Myles na gCopaleen (a.k.a. Flann O'Brien, Brian O'Nolan) showed, everybody would be *eabharaighbodaigh*.

Na gCopaleen describes the speech:

> There is scarcely a single word in the Irish ... that is simple and explicit. Apart from words with endless shades of cognate meaning, there are many with so complete a spectrum of graduated ambiguity that each of them can be made to express two directly contrary meanings, as well as a plethora of intermediate concepts that have no bearing on either. ... Superimpose on all that the miasma of ironic usage, poetic licence, oxy-

moron, plámás *[flattery]*, Celtic evasion, Irish bullery and Paddy Whackery, and it is a safe bet you will find yourself very far from home. [*Best of Myles*, reprinted by Dalkey Archive Press, Normal, Illinois, copyright 1968 Evelyn O'Nolan]

Another quote, this one from Mr Brundish in Penelope Fitzgerald's *The Bookshop:* "Understanding makes the mind lazy."

So don't fret. Put the book down and go back to your life. Read other books. Your experience of *Finnegans Wake*—however muddled—will resonate in the background: When you pick it up again you will probably hear a chord or two where only fragments were heard before.

King Roderick O'Conor — *pages 380–382*

Context. This passage ends the 3rd chapter of the 2nd part, in which Earwicker has been serving the customers at his public house, indulging in drink and story. Now they have been expelled for closing time, their ships cut loose upon the seas, and Earwicker is described in the character of Roderick O'Conor, the last high king of Ireland, during whose rule the Anglo-Normans invaded. In another ending of the Irish nation, Rory (Irish *Ruaidhrí*, whence the English "Roderick") O'Connor was a Fenian who held the Four Courts (now 5) in Dublin for a few months until they were destroyed; he was hanged in 1922 in reprisal for another shooting in the Civil War.

Pattern. Roderick is ⊓. The customers are 12. HCE becomes ⊔. S and K help him into his funeral ship, □.

Bowdler's Version.

> So anyhow, ... to wind up that longtobechronickled gettogether ... King Roderick O'Conor, ... when he found himself by himself in his grand old ... pile after all of them had all gone off ... to their castles of mud, ... well, what do you think he did, sir, ... he just went heeltapping through the winespilth and weevily popcorks that were kneedeep round his own ... round ... table, ... what did he go and do at all, ... with the wonderful midnight thirst was on him, as keen as mustard, ... if he did'nt go ... and suck up, ... in some ... cases with the assistance of his tongue, whatever surplus rotgut ... was left by the lazy lousers ... in the different bottoms of the various different ... drinking utensils ... no matter whether it was chateaubottled Guiness's or Phoenix brewery stout it was or John Jameson and Sons or Roob Coccola or, for the matter of that, O'Connell's famous old Dublin ale that he wanted like hell, ... of several different quantities and qualities ... till the rising of the morn, till that hen of Kaven's shows her beaconegg ... and all's set for restart after the silence, like his ancestors to this day after him (that the blazings of their ouldmouldy gods may attend to them we pray!), overopposides the cowery lad in the corner and forenenst the staregaze of the cathering candled, ... he came acrash a crupper sort of a sate on accomondation, whereuponce, ... heave hone, leave lone, ... a peerless pair, ever here and over there, with his fol the dee oll the doo on the flure of his feats and the feels of the fumes in the wakes of his ears ... he ... slumped to throne.

[49]

So sailed the stout ship *Nansy Hans*. From Liff away. For Nattenlaender. As who has come returns. Farvel, farerne! Goodbark, goodbye!

Now follow we out by Starloe!

Summary. This excerpt—amputated here of digression and elaboration—is quite easy to follow: King Roderick, left alone after playing host [communion, thanksgiving supper] to a party of drinkers, waded through the mess and drank what was left in all of their glasses. An ancestral thirst possessed him until morning. He crashed down sitting, and the servants ("the cowery lad" and "the cathering candled") heaved him into his throne. Settled thus, at the helm of his pub-ship, he sailed away through the night.

Comments. Here is the first sketch of the dreamer, the last of his kind (after this night, nothing will be the same), taking the thirsts of the world upon himself and letting the mess he leaves behind create a transformative dream.

THE KISS —*pages 383–386*

Context. This passage begins the 4th chapter of the 2nd part, after the collapse of Earwicker that we just read. He is now King Mark. In his dream he is Tristan. His ship is taking Tristan and Isolde from Ireland to Cornwall for her marriage to King Mark. Isolde's nurse provided a love potion to both instead of poison to the despairing Isolde.

Pattern. Tristan is ⌒ betraying Mark, ⊓, with Isolde, ⊣. The four listeners are the elderly chroniclers of ⊓'s history. The initials of Tristan, Isolde, and Mark spell Tim, Finnegan's name.

Bowdler's Version.

— *Three quarks for Muster Mark!*
Sure he hasn't got much of a bark
And sure any he has it's all beside the mark.
But O, Wreneagle Almighty, wouldn't un be a sky of a lark
To see that old buzzard whooping about for uns shirt in the dark
And he hunting round for uns speckled trousers around by Palmer-
   stown Park?
Hohohoho, moulty Mark!
You're the rummest old rooster ever flopped out of a Noah's ark
And you think you're cock of the wark.
Fowls, up! Tristy's the spry young spark
That'll tread her and wed her and bed her and red her
Without ever winking the tail of a feather
And that's how that chap's going to make his money and mark!

Overhoved, shrillgleescreaming. ... Seahawk, seagull, curlew and plover, kestrel and capercallzie. All the birds of the sea they trolled out rightbold when they smacked the big kuss of Trustan with Usolde.

And there they were too, when it was dark, whilest the wildcaps was circling, ... the winds aslight, ... listening in, as hard as they could, ... all four of them, all sighing and sobbing, and listening. Moykle ahoykling!

They were the big four, the four maaster waves of Erin, all listening, four. There was old Matt Gregory and then besides old Matt there was old Marcus Lyons, the four waves, and oftentimes they used to be saying grace together, right enough ...: here now we are the four of us: old Matt Gregory and old Marcus and old Luke Tarpey: the four of us and sure, thank God, there are no more of us: and, sure now, you wouldn't go and forget and leave out the other fellow and old Johnny MacDougall: the four of us and no more of us and so now pass the fish for Christ sake, Amen .... And so there they were, ... spraining their ears, luistening and listening to the oceans of kissening, with their eyes glistening, all the four, when he was kiddling and cuddling and bunnyhugging scrumptious his colleen bawn and dinkum belle, ... the hero, of Gaelic champion, the onliest one of her choice, her bleaueyedeal of a girl's friend, neither bigugly nor smallnice, meaning pretty much everything to her then, with his sinister dexterity, ... fore and aft, on and offsides, ... and cuddling her and kissing her, tootyfay charmaunt, in her ensemble of maidenna blue, with an overdress of net, tickled with goldies, Isolamisola, and whisping and lisping her about Trisolanisans, ... with his poghue like Arrahna-poghue, ... they all four remembered who made the world and how they used to be at that time in the vulgar ear cuddling and kiddling her, ... from under her mistlethrush and kissing and listening, in the good old bygone days of Dion Boucicault, the elder, in Arrah-na-pogue, in the otherworld of the passing of the key of Two-tongue Common, with Nush, the carrier of the word, and with Mesh, the cutter of the reed, ... when they were all four collegians on the nod, ... raising hell while the sin was shining, with their slates and satchels, playing Florian's fables and communic suctions and vellicar frictions with mixum members, ... and paying a pot of tribluts to Boris O'Brien, the buttler of Clumpthump, ... to see the mad dane ating his vitals. Wulf! Wulf! ... It brought the dear prehistoric scenes all back again, as fresh as of yore, Matt and Marcus, natural born lovers of nature, in all her moves and senses, and after that now there he was, that mouth of mandibles, vowed to pure beauty, and his Arrah-na-poghue, when she murmurously, after she let a cough, gave her firm order, if he wouldn't please mind, for a sings to one hope a dozen of the best favourite lyrical national blooms in Luvillicit, though not too much, reflecting on the situation, drinking in draughts of purest air serene and revelling in the great outdoors, before the four of them, in the fair fine night, whilst the stars shine bright, ... and he poghuing and poghuing like the Moreigner bowed his crusted hoed ... and there they were, ... listening, ... as tired as they were, the three jolly topers, with their mouths watering, all the four, the old connubial men of the sea, Luke and Johnny MacDougall and all wishening for anything at all of the bygone times, ... for a cup of kindness yet, for four farback tumblerfuls of woman squash, with them, all four, listening and spraining their ears for the millennium and all their mouths making water.

Summary. Three triplets and a quatrain satirically announce the imminent eclipse of immanent old King Mark by his trusted young knight Tristan. The verses were the cries ("quarks") of seabirds about the kiss of Tristan and Isolde. And listening in as well are the four masters and waves of Ireland—Matt, Marcus, and Luke, oh, and Johnny—with their white heads and clearing their throats in the Sea of Moyle [where Lir's children sang as swans until "the man from the north marries the woman from the south"] ("Moykle ahoykling"). They were straining to listen when he (Tristan) was cuddling his belle (Isolde, Iseult-la-Belle), bringing to mind the melodramas of 19th-century Irish playwright Dion Boucicault, especially *Arrah-na-Pogue* ["Arrah of the Kiss," in which Arrah gives her foster-brother Beamish Mac Coul the plans to free him from Wicklow Gaol on a rolled-up piece of paper hidden in her mouth when she kisses him; Arrah is engaged to Shaun the Post, who says, "that's the only post-office I mean to get my letters from the rest of my life"]. The four remembered as well their college years and such oral passing of the key with Nush, the carrier of the word [Shaun the Post], and with Mesh, the cutter of the reed [Shem the Penman—from *Jim the Penman*, a 19th-century play by Charles Young]. Isolde then asked Tristan to sing some popular songs. ["Sings to one hope a dozen of the best" is one of the recurring echoes of "six of one half a dozen of the other" that are heard—with several other phrases similarly echoing—through the book.] "Though not too much," she warned, and the four old men were wishing for their old times, for a taste, another (crushed-fruit) drink for woman's kindness yet.

Comments. This is an endearing picture of youth and age, leaving behind in their different ways, with blithe disregard, the accomplished King Mark. The young couple think only of themselves and each other. The elders think only of their own youth. At sea, the sleeper no longer haunts them. History for the moment is not a nightmare, though violence still lurks, but a sentimental farce.

St. Kevin and the Bath — *pages 604–606*

Context. This passage is part of the last chapter of the book. St. Kevin (who died in 618) lived for 7 years as a hermit in the cliffs of Glendalough (Valley of Two Lakes, where later were established 7 churches) in the Wicklow Mountains south of Dublin. He was chased there by the smitten lady Kathleen, who fell or was pushed to her death in one of the lakes.

Pattern. Kevin is an inward-looking ⌐ as opposed to Tristan's outgoing ⌐. He purifies himself in his purified triune mama sister bride, △, the river water.

Bowdler's Version.

Of Kevin, of increate God the servant, of the Lord Creator a filial fearer, who, given to the growing grass, took to the tall timber, ... shearing aside the four wethers and passing over the dainty daily dairy and dropping by the way the lapful of live coals and smoothing out Nelly Nettle and her lad of mettle, full of stings, fond of stones, friend of gnewgnawns bones and leaving all the messy messy to look after our douche douche, the miracles, death and life are these.

... Procreated on the ultimate ysland of Yreland ..., come their feast of precreated holy whiteclad angels, ... voluntarily poor Kevin, having been graunted the pravilege of a priest's postcreated portable *altare cum balneo*, ... in celibate matrimony at matin chime arose and westfrom went and came ... to our own midmost Glendalough-le-vert by archangelical guidance where amiddle of meeting waters of river Yssia and Essia river on this ... lone navigable lake piously Kevin, lawding the triune trishagion, amidships of his conducible altar super bath, rafted centripetally, ... midway across the subject lake surface to its supreem epicentric lake Ysle, ... whereupon with beached ... bath *propter* altar, with oil extremely anointed, accompanied by prayer, holy Kevin bided till the third morn hour to build a rubric penitential honeybeehivehut in whose enclosure to live in fortitude, ... whereof the arenary floor, most holy Kevin excavated as deep as to the depth of a seventh part of one full fathom, which excavated, venerable Kevin, taking counsel, proceded towards the lakeside of the ysletshore whereat seven several times he ... at sextnoon collected ... water sevenfold and with ambrosian eucharistic joy of heart as many times receded, carrying that privileged altar *unacumque* bath, which severally seven times into the cavity excavated ... then effused thereby letting there be water where was theretofore dry land,

... who now, confirmed a strong and perfect christian, blessed Kevin, exorcised his holy sisterwater, perpetually chaste, so that, well understanding, she should fill to midheight his tubbathaltar, most blessed Kevin, ninthly enthroned, whereamid, when violet vesper vailed, Saint Kevin, Hydrophilos, having girded his sable *cappa magna* as high as to his cherubical loins, at solemn compline sat in his sate of wisdom, that handbathtub, whereverafter, recreated *doctor insularis* of the universal church, keeper of the door of meditation, memory *extempore* proposing and intellect formally considering, recluse, he meditated continuously with seraphic ardour the primal sacrament of baptism or the regeneration of all man by affusion of water. Yee.

Summary. This passage is chock full of church ritual and lists of angelic ranks and other things sevenly as Kevin (described in seven progressively exalted terms—from "voluntarily poor" to "Saint") prepares his purified and purifying bath (in seven stages). In the invocatory first paragraph, he steps over the milk bottles at his door to leave the path of self-scourging and suffering (nettlesome and messy) for the more comfortable life of cool and clean ("douche douche") communion with nature—nature, however, remade to his desire.

With a portable combination altar-bath [I suppose by turning it over for each purpose in turn], Kevin arose before dawn ("matin") and guided by angels to Glendalough to the meeting of two rivers [⊣⊢; where they create a Y—notice all the Y's in the text, as in "ysland of Yreland"]. In his altar-bath, Kevin rafted midway across the lake where the rivers meet to the island in its center. At dawn ("prime"), with his bath-altar beached, Kevin anointed himself and prayed, waiting until nine o'clock ("third morn hour") to build a penitent's hut [a beehive hut characteristic of a Celtic recluse]. He dug out the sandy floor to a depth of one seventh of a fathom [about 10 inches]. At noon ("sextnoon"), he collected water from the shore with his altar-bath, carrying it seven times to fill the excavated bath floor. Thus having proved his grace he blessed the water and half-filled his tub-altar with it, where Kevin sat espoused and enthroned at three o'clock ("ninthly"). By evening ("vesper"), he had tied his robe up and at night ("compline") still sat in his bath, his seat of wisdom, carefully considering what his memory proposes—meditating thus on the regenerative quality of water.

Comments. Kevin is transformed by dedicating himself to the triune water (Y, the invagination of △). He shuns the world of pain and misery and ensconces himself in the belly of the water-filled earth. He weds himself thus to his image of the mother. The necessary rituals through which he approaches this blessed state are shaped by 7's, i.e., by the 7 visible "planets"—Sun, Moon, Mars, Mercury, Jupiter, Venus, Saturn—that define the 7 celestial spheres around the earth whence derive and echo the 7 canonical hours of the day (and virtues and sacraments and angelic orders and church hierarchies &c.) that mark Kevin's progress. There are also 7 liturgical colors, like the 7 colors of the rainbow—reflecting the 7 colors of the planets; color is the theme of the next passage we will look at. As Kevin here tames time to a meditative stillness, to civilize Ireland for a new dawn, Patrick will tame color for the 7-degree'd druid.

Archdruid Berkeley & St. Patrick—*pages 611–612*

Context. This passage is another part of the last chapter of the book. It describes the contest of wisdom between Patrick and king Leary's Druid (i.e., chief poet), from which Patrick won the right to preach throughout the kingdom (*see* History, *above*). George Berkeley (1685–1752) thought that our belief in natural order comes from the order of our perceiving mind and therefore of the similar mind that created and is in nature. He went on to assert that nothing exists except as perceived in the mind of God, that our perception of reality is in fact a sharing in the thoughts of God, an appropriate explanation in the world of a dream.* Berkeley's problem with the extramental world plays by pun into the excremental theme of *Finnegans Wake*.† He appears here as the ultimate philosopher of Ireland. His argument is presented in Pidgin English to suggest an oriental quality in Berkeley's thought as well as the effort to make him understood. Berkeley uses Chinese, Greek, and Latin words, and Patrick uses Latin, German, and Japanese (from the land of the rising sun). There are plays with the L-R interchange common in Irish as well as Oriental languages, and with the P-Q sound split between Britonnic and Gaelic: For example, Berkeley is Belkelly (among other efforts) and Patrick is Patholic. On the preceding page, we hear that Leary has bet half his crown

---

*Zeno of Elea may also play a part in the passage. Famous for his paradoxes, he elaborated the one-many opposition in the dogma of Parmenides, "The Ent is, the non-Ent is not" (as the 11th edition of *Encyclopedia Britannica* has it, and which the archdruid ("numpa one puraduxed seer") in this passage refers to as the "wisdom of Entis-Onton" [Latin being–Greek beings]): What is (Greek *on*) is, what is not is not. The first, the one, is the object of thought, indivisible, continuous, and perfect, whereas the second, the many, is the mutable object of sensation, everything commonly called reality, and does not exist— it is but a reflection of the one as perceived through the senses. Thus the archdruid claims to see the true reality inside what he sees, the light that is not reflected.

†Another pun-pair is word/turd. The transaccidentating artist-alchemist transforms shit into gold, expelled reality to outward symbols of inner life, or, akin to the agriculturalist, manure into food. The challenge of reading is not to see through the veil of printed words to something hidden but to transubstantiate them as symbols back to originating thought.

2 FABLES

These two fables apparently arose—and certainly took shape—in response to Wyndham Lewis's criticism of Joyce's *Work in Progress* (as *Finnegans Wake* was called while excerpts were being published—James and Nora kept the title secret until publication). Lewis was vehemently opposed to the unrational art of the age, exemplified, he thought, by Joyce's work, which he said wallowed in the flux of time, having no rational basis or goal. Lewis was also a snob, dismissing Joyce—when not attacking him for bringing down European civilization—as just a middle-class Irishman. Despite his vitriolic opinions, Lewis clearly considered Joyce's work worth troubling himself about, and Joyce admired Lewis's work, respecting him as a serious writer. They drank together whenever Lewis was in Paris. Both of them were born in 1882, a coincidence that Joyce considered quite significant. (Another example of this was Joyce's closeness to James Stephens, the Irish poet born on the same day as Joyce: When criticism against *Work in Progress* grew strong, Joyce, with his health and energy—if not his craft—ebbing, started preparing for Stephens to finish the book.)

The issues in these fables are crystallized in Lewis as an advocate of spatial perception—rationality, clarity, absolute truths—and Joyce as the avatar of temporal perception—impulsiveness, ambiguity, relativity (in morals as well as in the new physics of Einstein and Heisenberg). It is also expressed as dogmatism versus humanism. Having been educated by Jesuits, Joyce knew tyranny (and its attractions) when he saw its rumblings. These fables were first written in the 1920s; in the next decade, Joyce saw immediately the inherent evil in Hitler's rise to power, while his friends Wyndham Lewis and Ezra Pound saw a lot of good. By the time Hitler began his war, Lewis had realized his mistake.

The rivalry is characterized by eye and ear: one of them thinking he sees things as they are, the other only hearing things as they change. The eye-character (∧), ironically it seems at first, is known as a fine singer. But his repertoire is limited to popular songs. Against these melodic expressions of simple sentiment, the ear-character (⊏) hears a more complex rhythm in his soul, and expresses it in literature, a medium that straddles, ⊓-like, the visual and the auditory. Doing so to the extreme that he does, ⊏ subverts the stability of the word, which ∧ reveres as an inviolable edifice. ⊏ keeps the word alive.

THE MOOKSE AND THE GRIPES (pp. 152–159)

The tale of the Mookse and the Gripes is told by Shaun in the character of Professor Loewy-Brueller to illustrate how hopelessly primitive Shem is. A fox is portrayed as a moocow and a bit of a mouse (∧, Shaun), and the grapes as a bundles of gripes, filled with alcohol (⊏, Shem). They are opposing aspects of the Celtic pope and exile, Nicholas Breakspear, who as Adrian IV "gave" Ireland (by the bull *Laudabiliter*) to Henry II to civilize.

The Mookse sits on a stone while trying to convince the Gripes—who is gripping the branch of an elm tree across the stream—of his primacy, the primacy of space over time in the fabric of the universe. He consults his books. Between them, Nuvoletta (⊣) overlooks the stream, in which she sees her reflection (⊢). The Mookse and the Gripes in their disputation over who is the image of the father neither see nor hear her. Dusk falls, and the 2 men become pieces of laundry—the Mookse an apron, the

Gripes a handkerchief—spread out and hung out to dry and now gathered up by washerwomen. Nuvoletta, left alone, leaps from her tower and becomes her tear, one of the thousand and one that make the stream into a river.

The Ondt and the Gracehoper (pp. 414–419)

The fable of the Ondt and the Gracehoper is told by Shaun as he begins his midnight mail route. The narrator wants him to sing but he prefers to tell a moral tale. La Fontaine's ant and cricket (or Aesop's ant and fly) are transformed by Shaun's Norwegian self: "Ondt" meaning hard (∧) and "Gracehoper" from the Norwegian *graeshoppe.* The stern and solemn Ondt is the winter sun, strong when the happy-go-lucky Gracehoper—the summer sun—is weak. The dominant one frolics with and is attended by 4 insect-girls—Floh (flea), Luse (louse), Bienie (bee), and Vespatilla (wasp)—representing the cardinal points of the sky. The passage is abuzz with the names of insects and their parts.

The tale begins with a description of the Gracehoper in his ascendance. He fiddles away happily jumping about. He tries to seduce the 4 insect-girls in his cottage called Tingsomingenting (from Danish: "thing like no thing"). At the wake for his father he leads the dancing, adding to the songs about the great one songs about his insect-girls. But he is but one son of the fallen father. The Ondt is shunning their company, filling up his home—"windhame," for Wyndham Lewis—called Nixnixundnix ("snow snow and snow"—from Latin) in anticipation of winter. The Ondt prays for protection and long life.

While the Ondt is secure in his space, the Gracehoper, having indulged in love and debt, is broke, sick, and very hungry. All around he hears "Nichtsnichtsundnichts" (nothing nothing and nothing*). As winter sets in, he has eaten up all of his time. At Christmastime (solstice—the turning of the year back towards summer) he wanders in circles around his house in a delirium, in

---

*Both instances pun on old Greek *nyx*, night.

the blizzard that mocks him (when it's winter in the northern hemisphere, it's summer in the south).

Then the Gracehoper puts his faith in time ("tossed himself in the vico" [as many an Irish hero placed himself in a small boat to let the waves carry him whither they will]) and sees the Ondt—enthroned with the insect-girls nibbling at his body, enjoying the "Thingsumanything" he had saved for. Then the Ondt sees the wasted Gracehoper, the image of despair, at his door. The Ondt, basking in his riches, offers his hospitality but makes it clear what he thinks the Gracehoper's place is, namely, as a beggar before his material glory.

The promised song wraps up the fable: With the Ondt laughing too hard, the Gracehoper forgives the Ondt's reproof, accepting the truth of his want. The Gracehoper continues to express his debt to his brother the Ondt in his time of need, and asks if either can exist without the other. A place to love, a time to kiss (*A locus to loue, a term it t'embarass*—locust and termite, too): These are what drive (or enclose—*tick*) the common man, as North seeks South and the Occident the Orient, round and round. Before the insect-girls leave the Ondt (*your mocks*—Mookse) for *my gropes* (Gripes), sings the Gracehoper, *An extense must impull, an elapse must elopes*, i.e., space will look inward and time fly and—take that!—the sick are well. As I see by your sight, the Gracehoper continues, hark what I hear. You see me thin but unbroken on the broadness of your works; in my laughable universe you'd hardly find such meat as your left behind. You're large, you straddle the world, you stretch to the heavens (*Your genus its worldwide, your spacest sublime!*), but *why can't you beat time?*

And so the Gracehoper reclaims the song—Shem wrote what Shaun sings—because the Ondt can feed them and his banknotes shine clear but he can't hold the beat. Time will take him, too.

The Fables of La Fontaine

The Fox and the Grapes

A certain fox of Gascony, though others say of Normandy,
Dying of hunger, saw, at the top of a trellis
Some grapes, all ripe appearing
And covered in rosy skin.
The gentle fox would gladly have a meal
But because he couldn't reach them:
They're too green, he said, and only good for boors.
Didn't he make things better by complaining?

The Ant and the Cricket

The cricket, having sung
All summer long, was very unprepared
When winter winds arrived:
She found not one little morsel
Of a fly or even a worm.
She went to cry about her hunger
To the ant her neighbor,
Begging her to lend her
Some seeds to survive
To the next season.
I will pay you, she said,
By August, have faith,
The interest and the principal.
The ant is not so generous
(That's her smallest fault):
What did you do when it was warm?
She said to her neighbor's prayers.
—Night and day, to all who came,
I sang, don't be so angry.
—You sang! That makes me glad.
And so! You now must dance.

ALP

"Anna Livia Plurabelle" is the last chapter of part I. Joyce was recorded reciting the last few pages of it—it's a good way to hear the sound of *Finnegans Wake*, in his chant-like delivery. In this chapter, two washerwomen are gossiping across the river Liffey. Their talk follows the course of the river, and they grow farther apart from each other.

196–201
Viking settlement at pool where the Dodder enters the Liffey

They begin with HCE's sin, the ravaging of ALP, the sea trader making landfall, sailing his bark right up her and her rushing to meet him—He was a gloomy old man, and she was bringing him breakfast till she was worn out and he would cast it away with scorn. Then she would sing of her love to his deaf ears. Then she taught passing girls and paid them to go in to him. Her song laments their current stasis and poverty but admits the comfort of her bed else she'd rush away to feel the sea wind blowing into her.

201–204
The Liffey's origin on Mt Kippure in Wicklow

Her 111 children and former lovers: The first was long before a countryman of Kildare fell a great oak across her slim body, it was back in Wicklow before she ever dreamed of the city or ocean, a hermit plunged his anointed hands into her streaming hair and a rainbow round her drew him on to raise her cool water to his lips, and before that two lads in short britches went through her before she had a bosom or a hair at her fanny, and before that she was licked by a hound, but first of all she slipped out by the gap and lay in the pools of rain wriggling in laughter for the first blush of spring.

204–205	The narrative is interrupted to comment on some dirty and torn drawers.
205–209 Tidal estuary	Her past was published and everyone mocked HCE, so ALP had a plan to get even: She borrowed the sack and lamp off

her son Shaun the Post and went out in disguise. She let down her hair and bathed and oiled and perfumed herself, wove a garland for her hair, made anklets and bracelets and a necklace of stones and shells, painted her face, and sent her two maids into the city to request a meeting and forth she came. Her appearance: short, plowman's clogs, peaked hat with streamers, eyeglasses, veil, earring, speckled stockings, calico chemise, orange knickers, &c., a clothespin on her nose, and she was chewing something and her skirt trailed 50 miles behind her. What a sight!

209–212 Flood	What's in her bag? Gifts for all of her 1001 children—all the things given her in their dreams—and they all run to her, because

she has something of each of them, including on Issy love in the future and from Shem the past.

212–215 The waters dissipate into the sea	The story breaks to borrow soap (the washerwomen are now quite far apart) and comment on the reading material left in a priest's cassock. Dusk: The dark blends

them into the tree and stone they spread the laundry on—They are starting to have trouble hearing each other; and it's getting cold and the wind is up. Where are all her children now? Some here, more no more, more again lost alla stranger. One of the washerwomen thinks she sees HCE on the white horse of the sun and ALP as golden Isis. The other complains of how hard and long she toils, and sees the four old men and their ass. The other sees a light—lighthouse, fireboat, burning bush, or returning love?—and knows they must part to meet again.

215–216 Anna Livia and Dear Dirty Dublin—our first father and dam, with us still in their daughters and sons, the same anew. Anna was, Livia is, Plurabelle's to be. The washerwomen have not gone home, they are stone and stem, Shaun and Shem. The rivering waters, night overtakes them.

HCE

Four old men, representing the provinces of Ireland, are atop a (burial) mound fiddling with a radio (like Osiris's coffin) from which HCE speaks—often stammering—first defending himself against the charge of visiting prostitutes, as well as defending ALP against the suggestion that she was one so visited.

532-533. HCE [Adam calling from Amsterdam] swears by his wife that he is a clean-living man, that he was never guilty of crime against any young girl and should have her arrested as a prostitute were she but thinking of such a thing ("tinkling of such a tink"). He has a dream wife for all that.

533-534. She has incomparably ("incompatibly") small feet [like a paleolithic fertility figurine, and Cinderella]. The chaplain can speak of his clean character, even when he introduced her to the four-poster chamber music in their home sweet home, reminding the listeners that he intended when young to enter the church—ask Michael Engels. The transmission breaks up.

534-535. The voice returns, calm, more assertive, still stammering. He has nothing to hide, could consult solicitors to prevent publication of libel by low cads to any high personage. The cad stumbled away drunk from HCE's inns—shame on the cur's lying soul! May he never see his face again! It was he who faced his ma-ma-majesty ("ecclesency," priest-king) who came to his own property on horseback. He curses the lowness of the cad some more. Enough!

535–536. A self-pitying voice takes over—Old Whitehowth, 39 years old. He asks a dear lady to judge him by the fruits of the tree he gave her—their 2 daughters and 3 sons, as represented on the city's coat of arms. O pity a poor father!

The transmission continues as a seance: HCE says that was someone else's voice, a spirit in retired exile. But he will not let that other bear his burdens.

536–540. He says he has bared himself on both sides, sentence him at all and he will protest if it does not occur again [a revealing slip of construction, one of many by which he seems to want to be punished]. He tells his listeners he is Irish, sworn and witnessed, his sun in the west. He will pay the fair price for any misconduct and discontinue same, denying any part in it, as it is now told to him that a quarter-brother who sometimes stands in for him was seen with a slave girl HCE sold his part in. He's a married man, a woman is sacred. He is not the kind of ass to bray at pictures of girls in frocks. Not interested. Why shouldn't he be? Improbable! To have bought or sold same: "Utterly improperable!" And there is the chance of disease.

Absurd! To buy a woman like a fish at market—he wouldn't even know how. There was a man resembling him: Deucollion. He played the trick. HCE will swear his own naked innocence, thinking of the generally admired poet Dante-Goethe-Shakespeare. He does penance and keeps up his payments. The amusing part is that since he placed his residence here among stranger and enemy—then a bog, now a magnificent city—here where his tenure of office and his toils of domestication first began, English famine and epidemics have left this land "and notorious naughty livers are found not on our rolls." His city is "pleasant, comfortable and wholesome." Hills are nearby, as are fields. There is the river ("Libnia Labia") for fresh water. The sea is at hand.

The four listeners chant travel slogans urging a visit to Drumcollogher [Dublin, *see* Geography].

540–545. "Things are not as they were." Where battles were fought now the bus stops for shopping, all on him, the sleeping giant, happy town, in good hands now, the devils gone, all are free. HCE boasts, enumerating what he has made himself: domes, towers, coinage. He was Daniel in the lion's den, the Viking (Lochlann) that slew Brian Boru, &c., faced the 3 peepers and 2 beauties, spun night music for slumber while strife threatened from the east, raised potatoes and berries, heard and saw everything and said it out loud, won followers and fumers, gave food to the tired, promoted the whole man, multiplied his boundary to Australia (Botany Bay) and America (Yanks), has been receiving letters and petitions calling for song, has secretly built for more open repose, disclosing the domestic scene: "fair home overcrowded ... respectable ... night soil has to be removed through snoring household ... inherited silk hat from father-in-law ... respectability unsuccessfully aimed at"—let them all come to his town. And he grants them liberty and ownership.

545–546. He has struggled long for his people and the protection of his law, agrarian and civil, over all the dark forces. His lord has given him arms, which he describes [the motto (initials H. C. E.) means "yesterday, tomorrow, even today"]. It is idle to inquire which of his sundered parts he is, naked or clothed, he is all at once ("simultaneous"). Till the end of the show.

The listeners make sure they have put in enough money to hear more.

546–550. The voice continues. "Annoyin part of it was," he says, had the river (his faithful wife) gone uphill or left her bed, one might ask where her deceivers were. Yet she swears no such thing happened, and he agrees, for she always followed what was fair. Even so, he loved her. And she wept. The listeners are moved.

HCE describes taking his delights with her, riding a raft along her length, and he bade the sea retire from them [built sea walls], and he straddled her with bridges until he knew her with all his worshipping body (whore-shipping bawdy). Heaven thundered.

They were one. An iron band marked her as his, and a well attended ceremony of wedlock. [And so begins a long list of all he's done for his Irish love.] He girdled her [built quays] to enfranchise her freedom. He gave her many things for her new life in the city, luxuries and adornments. People had rest from their tormenters, the sod quaked no more, frozen loins were stirred and lived: peace, perfect peace. He hung up Christmas lights like a crown of pearls. He drank his fill of draught, whiskey, and port. He was a bad boy until he fled to the east. He settled the new world with "the little crither of my hearth," whom he charmed and plumped and gave her a good Cristmas show. Moral: Be sure to book.

The four listeners express their new respect.

550–552. And he fed her, and gave her toiletries, and devised evening games, with mayors and mayoresses watching them out of paintings, then a hymn and sleep, and dreams, for which he prepared the way. And he built for her a convenient and quiet earth closet. Didn't he fix his festivals? Wasn't he on Egyptian steles? Hadn't he been read through the ages ("hieros, gregos and demotocriticos")? Hadn't he 3 castles and 2 medals [bronze by gold?]? And had he not, by Ulysses, walked his Irish road to the way of Venus? He was popularly elected. He had 4 states extended. He set up opposing ministers in stone churches of refuge replacing wattle and mud, thy vault, O holy wisdom ("hereround is't holied!"). He pushed and pulled all. He clothed her maze (maize) by his 7 winding winds. He reformed her church with a fine bell, adding a shallow bath and flower boxes. And she sat her bare bottom ("chillybombom") on the altar stone [his erection].

The 4 old men chuckle (as they hail him).

552–554. And—Her Chastener Ever—he did teach ("learn") her in the wholehailed alphabet, with a raw switch. And he spread before his Livvy—where blood had blighted acres—mats of grass lawn [Phoenix Park], gardens of wonders, esplanades, statues, and temples, for any holiday schedule a pleasure walk. And he planted for his hot lass a bowered vineyard and villas and ponds for ducks, den, glen, valley, chase, hill, "with a magicscene wall." And he brewed for his alpine belle (who makes his head hot—"wig-warming wench") his porter, "the frothy freshener." And he lay himself down, welcomed all, and they all on their horses danced for her pleasure and she laughed as they kicked at the whip.

The 4 elders dissolve into her laughter.

༄

"every telling has a taling and that's the he and the she of it" (p. 212): ALP and HCE. In the landscape, they are river and city, specifically Dublin and the Liffey, murmuring outside the sleeper's shutter. In person they are mama and papa, life-givers, judges, forgivers, imperfect, forgiven. In time's universe, "Anna was, Livia is, Plurabelle's to be" (p. 214); she is fate, eternal cycle of dying and renewing. And HCE is the world ash, "Yggdrasselmann" (p. 88), whose branches hold up heaven* and roots are fed by springs in the three worlds: of gods, of men, of the dead. Every night, they build their dear city of God that it be laid desolate for morning.

---

*"The heaven tree of stars hung with humid nightblue fruit" *(Ulysses)*.

13 PASSAGES

Overture (pp. 3–4)

For this and the following passages, I continue the clumsy combination of paraphrase, explanation, and commentary to provide an impression that you can use towards your own reading. This first passage, the first four paragraphs of *Finnegans Wake*, is like the overture to an opera, sounding many of the motifs that will appear throughout: the river and Dublin, Howth and the park, doubling, women and men, Shem and Shaun and the fall of their father, their battles, the steps and arc of a rainbow, the sunset as a phoenix fire. Above all, it sounds the theme of cyclical time taking us backwards and forwards, the same anew, the rise after the fall. But not before the necessary drama.

The riverrun is the Liffey before it reaches Dublin, then as it flows past the Adam and Eve tavern or church which stands for Dublin itself, where opposites meet, and out past the shore into the bay, all of this where we've been before and will see again at Howth Castle and Environs (i.e., in HCE).

What is to be has already been, which this book will now review (it moves here from the present tense to the past). "And here are the details" (p. 611). Tristram of Brittany (neither the mythical nor the historical), in violet love, had not yet returned to take possession of Iseult or Howth peninsula. Peter Sawyer had not yet found his town by the Oconee river in Laurens County, Georgia, that he named after his mother city, Dublin. Nor a peat fire, nor a voice from afar answered Irish to Patrick's propositions. Soon had a goat been switched for the sacrifice of Isaac, Parnell had ousted Isaac Butt, Jacob had tricked his blind father (by his mother's direction, with goat dressed up as venison) to gain his blessing. Not yet were 2 Esthers wroth with 2-in-1 Jonathan Swift.

Then Shem or Shaun brewed their father malt (both of him and for him) by artificial light and the red end of his ("pre-electric" (p. 380)) reign was to be seen on the water (sunset). The thunderous fall of a once-respectable elder is often told through life and history.

This humpty-dumpty fall involved so suddenly Finnegan that his head in Howth sends a query in quest of his toes. Their place is at the hill in the park where Dublin—from the first—long has picnicked by the Liffey, and orange has battled green.

The head will, but the feet won't: All battles are raging in this Irish body, in the fight against sleep: cannibals and rebels, chance cuddles and ruined castles, prostitutes with priests, the straw man of empire with the strength of a lying tongue. He is sprawled by sin but his fame has filled the sky.

What is it? Iseult? The oak is now peat yet she (the elm—first woman in Norse myth) leaps in sleep from the ashes of his slaying (the ash is first man). As Finnegan succumbs to sleep, his dream-woman emerges like Eve out of Adam to tell him he will rise again: Before you know it the farce will finish and you will be out of this holy mess and back where it began in Phoenix Park.

Finnegan's Wake (pp. 4–6)

The rest of the first chapter is an elaboration of this song—and other "stage Irish" songs—with talk of the man, his fall, and the promise of his resurrection (although when a splash of whiskey does revive him, he is pushed back down to rest in peace (pp. 24–28)). He is examined like a prehistoric mound, a monument, a book (*see* The Book, *below*). Here is the old song itself, dating from 1850's America.

> Tim Finnegan lived in Walkin Street
> A gentleman Irish, mighty odd;
> He'd a beautiful tongue so rich and sweet
> And to rise in the world he carried a hod.
> Now Tim had a sort o' the tipplin' way
> With a love of the liquor poor Tim was born
> And to help him on with his work each day
> He'd a drop of the craythur ev'ry morn.
>
> *Chorus*
> Whack fol the dah now dance to your partner
> Welt the flure, your trotters shake;
> Wasn't it the truth I told you
> Lots of fun at Finnegan's wake!
>
> One mornin' Tim was rather full
> His head felt heavy which made him shake,
> He fell from the ladder and broke his skull
> And they carried him home his corpse to wake.
> They wrapped him up in a nice clean sheet
> And laid him out across the bed,
> With a gallon of whiskey at his feet
> And a barrel of porter at his head.
>
> His friends assembled at the wake
> And Mrs Finnegan called for lunch,
> First they brought in tea and cake
> Then pipes, tobacco and whiskey punch.
> Biddy O'Brien began to cry
> "Such a nice clean corpse, did you ever see?
> "Arrah, Tim, mavourneen, why did you die?"
> "Ah, hold your gab" said Paddy McGee!
>
> Then Biddy O'Connor took up the job
> "O Biddy," says she, "You're wrong, I'm sure":
> Biddy gave her a belt in the gob
> And left her sprawlin' on the floor.
> And then a mighty war did rage

> 'Twas woman to woman and man to man,
> Shillelagh law did all engage
> And the row and the ruction soon began.
>
> Then Mickey Maloney ducked his head
> When a naggin of whiskey flew at him,
> It missed, and fallin' on the bed
> The liquor scattered over Tim.
> Bedad he revives! See how he rises!
> Timothy rising from the bed,
> Says,"Whirl your whiskey around like blazes
> Thanam o'n Dhoul! D'ye think I'm dead?"

He was a master builder of long ago (who could put away the drink) and he put up piles of buildings by the river that he hugged for his little wife. In his favorite overalls and trowel in hand he calculated skyscrapers out of next to nothing, with "larrons o'toolers clittering up and tombles a'buckets clottering down."

One of the first to bear arms and a name (Giant Boozer). [Vico says that the first family crests were the plowed fields. Their cultivation is the image of rebirth after burial, the continually renewed supply of grain for brewing.]

What brought about his fall? To avoid libellous rumor, "cropherb the crunchbracken" (a sheep or goat in the graveyard) shall decide his worth. It might have been a bad brick or due to a collapse (his past caught up with him—there are 1001 stories). But as sure as Adam ate Eve's holy apple, one morning he was filled with drink and as the wall went up he went down. He was dead. His monument is there (here) for all to see.

It's a large fairy mound (*sidhe*, pronounced *shee*), and they wailed as for Finn Mac Cool. And for more drink ("Fillagain"). They all joined in by the dozen. They laid him down on his bed with a bottle of whiskey [water] at his feet and a barrel of Guinness [genesis] at his head. Himself hanging between.

THE BOOK (pp. 18–20)

Examination of the earth-book of the old parents' history continues at a letter-filled midden heap, reminding us of the passing of civilizations. Tools to fell trees and plow the field are found. Then like figures at battle that face off and fall, the Runic futhorc alphabet is carved. The use of objects for an alphabet becomes general—the tiny characters that stand for all. They are old and wobbly, some obsolete, and snakes are swarming through it although (or because) Patrick scotched them.

Notches for calculating are here, too, and more tales to tell about the numbers, particularly the group of 1-1-1, the infinite sons and daughters of the delta.

There was as yet no paper, and the pen like a mighty mountain still groaned to give birth to mice [*see* Aesop's fable]. Then were signs and speeches, but "the world, mind, is, was and will be writing its own wrunes for ever" on everything under our senses while the last man has still to tether his camel (*gimel*, the 3rd Hebrew letter) to her date palm [in which Osiris was hidden] and enter his tomb (i.e., till the cows come home). Cut and scrape and soak a ram's skin: paper, which then meets type. Every word carries 70 readings "throughout the book of Doublends Jined" (∞) till the door that opened closes it [the Greek letter *delta*, Δ, ALP's sign, comes from the Phoenician—the symbol was a door, as the Hebrew name *daleth* still means*; in the kabbalist Tarot, daleth corresponds to the mother, or empress; the corresponding Irish letter, *dair*, meaning "oak," as in Bridget's Kildare, "church of the oak," is coincidentally pronounced *dor*].

---

*ALP is the Hebrew spelling of the first letter, *aleph*, a glottal stop, the point from which all the letters and numbers flow: from *beth* to *tav* (the vaudeville team Butt & Taff in *Finnegans Wake*) and around again. The symbol whence aleph derives is the head of a cow, Io, the $\forall$-shaped head of Taurus whose red star once marked the new year at the spring equinox. Early Christians used the corresponding Greek letter alpha (α) to symbolize their piscine messiah, Jesus. Aleph null ($\aleph_0$) in set theory is equal to ω (*omega*, the last letter of the Greek alphabet), which is the size (count) of the set of natural numbers, or infinity; $\aleph_0$, however, is but the first in a series of increasing sizes of infinity. ALP is nothing and everything, the beginning and the end.

Slander (pp. 33–34)

Excerpt from Thomas Bowdler's *The Shorter Finnegans Wake:*

A baser meaning has been read into these characters the literal sense of which decency can safely scarcely hint. It has been blurtingly bruited by certain wisecrackers that he suffered from a vile disease. To such a suggestion the one selfrespecting answer is to affirm that there are certain statements which ought not to be, and one should like to hope to be able to add, ought not to be allowed to be made. Nor have his detractors, who, an imperfectly warmblooded race, apparently conceive him as a great white caterpillar capable of any and every enormity in the calendar, mended their case by insinuating that, alternately, he lay at one time under the ludicrous imputation of annoying Welsh fusiliers in the people's park. Hay, hay, hay! Hoq, hoq, hoq! Faun and Flora on the lea love that little old joq. To anyone who knew and loved the christlikeness of the big cleanminded giant H. C. Earwicker throughout his long vicefreegal existence the mere suggestion of him as a lustsleuth nosing for trouble in a boobytrap rings particularly preposterous. Truth compels one to add that there is said to have been some case of the kind implicating a quidam (if he did not exist it would be necessary to invent him) abhout that time stambuling haround Dumbaling in leaky sneakers who has remained anonymos but was, it is stated, posted at Mallon's at the instance of watch warriors of the vigilance committee and years afterwards seemingly waiting his turn for thatt chopp pah kabbakks alicubi on the old house. Lowe, you blondy liar, Gob scene you in the narked place and she what's edith ar home defileth these boyles! There's a cabful of bash indeed in the homeur of that meal. Slander, let it lie its flattest, has never been able to convict our good and great and no ordinary Southron Earwicker, that homogenius man, as a pious author called him, of any graver impropriety than that of having behaved with ongentilmensky immodus opposite a pair of dainty maidservants in the swoolth of the rushy hollow whither, or so the two gown and pinners pleaded, dame nature in all innocency had spontaneously and about the same hour of the eventide sent them both but whose published testimonies are, where not dubiously pure, visibly divergent on minor points touching the intimate nature of this, a first offence in vert or venison which was admittedly an incautious but, at its wildest, a partial exposure with such attenuating circumstances as an abnormal Saint Swithin's summer and a ripe occasion to provoke it.

"Alicubi" alludes to the Ka'aba at Mecca, the center of the world and symbol of the heavenly city—it is Earwicker's public house in Chapelizod.

THE BALLAD OF PERSSE O'REILLY (PP. 44–47)

The broadcast of calumny culminates here with the rann (verse) of Hosty, the song that justifies and confirms your man's fall. Join in and sing along, as the notes are provided.

rann 1. He is likened to Humpty Dumpty and wishfully to Oliver Cromwell. The Norse name Olaf (the founder of Dublin) is the origin of both Humphrey and Oliver. The Magazine Wall is in Phoenix Park, near the Liffey.

rann 2. As he's lost all respect, he'll be put into jail by the archbishop.

rann 3. His civic plans were overreaching.

rann 4. He failed because . . . he gave no milk!

rann 5. He made many products universally available for sale and was popularly considered a cheat.

rann 6. But now he's out of business, the lot to be burned as the bailiff seeks him.

rann 7. Damn the day that brought him to Dublin bay.

rann 8. His name and accent are mocked.

rann 9. He imposed himself on a native maid.

rann 10. It's embarrassing, uncivilized, sexual.

rann 11. Riding in Phoenix Park, someone opened the window and he was caught in the crossfire (or the wind gave him a cold, or the guards caught him up).

rann 12. Won't his missus clean out his ears!

rann 13. A rally is promised to send him to the devil.

rann 14. And he'll never get back up again (fragmentation but no reunification, which hope HCE will proceed to defy). Cromwell evicted Catholic landowners to Connacht or hell.

Agricultural Cain, after murdering his more favored pastoral brother Abel, became a city-builder.

In the name of free Ireland, Hosty supports the actions of the British powers (His Worship, fusiliers) against the Dane. He is perhaps their agent, as his name suggests (from Latin *hostis*, foreigner). This is akin to the Norman promotion in England of King Arthur stories to unite conqueror and conquered against the earlier conqueror, the Anglo-Saxons.

Letter (pp. 104–108)

First an invocation, and then 123 of the many names her work has gone by, the *"First and Last Only True Account ... by a Woman of the World who only can Tell Naked Truths about a Dear Man"* (p. 107), e.g., *"As Tree is Quick and Stone is White So is My Washing done by Night."* Now follows some puzzlement over the shape-shifting many-sided script itself (it is supposed that she did not write herself). It was once assumed to be the work of a drunken congenital criminal. A bird ("Oriolopos") might think the marks are insects and chase them like butterlies ("vanessas") from flower to flower, line to line. Several Arabic words (according to McHugh's *Annotations*) might be detected in the text, from an effort to thus interpret the scrawl.

kidooleyoon	*kidout'iun*, science
madernacerution	*madenakrout'iun*, literature
	(made to sound like chewing)
lour	news
herou	far
kitchernott	*kišer*, night
hasard	*hazar*, 1000
Zerogh	*zereg*, day
pon	owl
giaours	non-Muslims (Turkish)
aysore	*aysor*, today
Amousin	husband

Notice that Joyce often puts an English hint—if not the actual translation—along with a foreign word: "madernacerution of lour lore is rich," "kitchernott darkness," "hasard and worn" (i.e., 1001), "on till Zerogh hour" (i.e., till dawn, when the sun rises like an egg, whence the sign for *zero*, 0), "pon owl," "aysore today." This is also an example of how allusions and languages are generally clustered in a meaningful way rather than randomly scattered.

The attempt to see Arabic in it is, however, given up—"Amousin though not but" (i.e., not quite there). Closer inspection reveals inevitable crimes inflicted on the document by several personalities. And, in conclusion, just as contraries coalesce under closed eyes, so by battles society bumps along by letters ("ox-househumper" representing the Hebrew/Phoenician A-B-C) the long lane of generations.

SHEM (pp. 169–172)

The chapter (pp. 126–168) preceding this section is generally considered as a look through the family album with 12 questions and answers. The 11th answer is an apology by Shaun contrasting his glorified self to the "primitive" Shem, and the 12th question affirms the judgement: "*Sacer esto?*" (He is cursed?). But the answer is a defiant "We are Shem": "*Semus sumus!*" This next chapter examines "his lowness." It ends with Shem mimicking the voice of their mother: Where Shaun condemned, Shem gives voice to the silenced. The "ALP" chapter discussed above then follows.

"Shemus" is an anglicized spelling of the Irish form of "James," which is a diminutive of "Jacob." Shem is the son of Noah and father of the Semites. *Shem* (or *sham* or *sh'm*) is the Hebrew word for "name," particularly of the creator, who—according to the Kabbalah—from the spirit of his name made the alphabet, and the universe, through air, water, and fire, the 3 mother letters *aleph*, *mem*, and *shin*. The Irish vocative (calling) form of Shem, *A Ham*, links him to Noah's cursed son, Ham, the father of Africans. Adaline

Glasheen says that Shem's crime in Shaun's view has been to betray the interests of white supremacy.

The second paragraph of this chapter describes his appearance, which is so imperfect, sickly and thin, that even Shem himself as a child recognized that he was not a man, that he is a sham,* triumphant in that knowledge.† The next paragraph confirms that Shem would not eat or drink like a man, preferring, for example, cheap tinned salmon to the real thing fresh, no slabs of beef aswim in gravy, and Europe's lentil hash to Ireland's "split little pea." And instead of whiskey or beer he sobbed into some sort of sour grape juice which he drank more than enough of and called—to the horror of his guests—the piss of an archduchess, Fanny Urinia.

The fourth paragraph (p. 171) claims you can see the lowness oozing out of him in a shipboard photograph taken when he repudiated the nation—the girl who snapped it knew by his gipsy tongue he was a "bad fast man." Lest we forget about him, Johns the butcher (his liver a spatiality) inserts an ad (or "communication," in contrast to that on p. 181). Every good ad has an extra level of meaning to draw the attention—as Leopold Bloom has taught us—and this one excommunicates the inadequately carnivorous brother.

SHEM THE PENMAN (pp. 182–186)

Shem, the son of Noah, gave his name to alchemy, the practice of material transmutation, most dramatically of feces and earth to the sun's gold. It is occult science at its most hermetic, mercury (Hermes) being the essential element of its processes. Here is a portrait of our Shem resorting to alchemy in order to write (an activity invented by Thoth, the Egyptian Hermes).

Scham is German for vulva. There is a "Madonna with Child" by Bellini (in the Academia Carrara di Belli Arti, Bergamo) in which Jesus's shirt is lifted to reveal labia (lips) instead of a penis and testicles. The Hebrew *'asham*, means "to be guilty."
†"Sham" in German is *schein*. *Schein* also means "splendor."

The house was filthy and stank, littered with all manner of scraps—notes, food, clothing, including the garters of all kinds of women, and himself among the broken furniture. He prepared eggs for himself in a closet by chanting magic formulas to guide the interaction of white and yolk, adding a host of supporting material to the concoction. He was in need of space. When he was refused supplies at the stationers, he made his own ink and paper. The process is described in Latin (p. 185) to save a priest from blushing, although the English interjections sum it up: With his bared buttocks close to the earth, weeping and groaning he evacuated into his hand, then, free from the black beast, he put it into a burial urn where he urinated, chanting in a loud voice, "My tongue is the pen of a swift scribe &c." [Psalm 45, a song of praise to a princess], and then from the mixture, cooked, exposed to cold, he made himself indelible ink.

With this obscene matter, heated up, he "wrote over every square inch of the only foolscap available, his own body" (p. 185),* till the skin by that corrosive influence unfolded "all ... cycle-wheeling history ...†

> reflecting from his own individual person life unlivable, trans-accidentated through the slow fires of consciousness into a dividual chaos, perilous, potent, common to allflesh, human only, mortal [p. 186]

Each word took its toll, and he waned away, circling the square for his last public appearance when the crowd turned to lynch him like he was a drunk Parnell, but a blond cop saw it was ink that blackened his skin.

---

* 'We called him a Poet: is not his body the (stuffed) parchment-skin 'whereon he writes, with cunning Huddersfield dyes, a Sonnet to his 'mistress' eyebrow?' (Carlyle, *Sartor Resartus*).
† Vico's giants, whence history flows, grew so large after the flood because they were let as babies to play in their own filth, absorbing the nitrous salts. They grew stronger penetrating the dense forests (which they fertilized with their continuing filth) without fear of gods, fathers, and teachers.

The Song of the Four (pp. 398–399)

The 4 chroniclers, after witnessing the kiss of Tristan and Isolde, and recalling in turn past romances, sing a love song to Isolde, princess of Ireland. They keep the usual order of Matthew-Mark-Luke-John, N-S-E-W, Ulster-Munster-Leinster-Connacht, a cross (whereas in the chapter that this song ends they spoke in circular order, W-S-E-N).

Matthew sings with brotherly jealousy.
Mark sings worshipfully of a queen born of the sea.
Luke sings as an old love and true friend.
John sings in the excitement of success in love.

We leave the 4 to go on with their keg down the river and end part II.

Vision of Shaun (pp. 403–405)

Part IV begins with bells chiming the hour . . . 6? no . . . 12. A snoring arch hump of a man is seen, and then his wife, and someone is watching them, reader—so the light is switched out.

The ass ("I, poor ass" (p. 405)) of the 4 annalists continues his narration, that as he passed by dozing in the dark by the river where it seemed that laundry lay by he heard with the midnight chimes "vixen's laughter" (p. 403) and a "broadtone" (p. 404) and thought all the earth cried "Shaun! Shaun! Post the post" and that he rose in answer: first the glow of his lamp then the lad himself growing before him in grand dress—"everything the best"—and the colors of Ireland spilling down his front in peas, rice, and egg-yolk and the letters R. M. D.: Shaun himself.

Farewell to Haun (pp. 471–473)

Part III, which Joyce called "∧abcd," has seen Shaun the Post, Jaun the Boast (Don Juan), who leaves his sister in the care of Dave the Dancekerl, and now Haun, a more Gaelic pronunciation of his name, to wish him well on his way. He is invoked for his singing, his departure is grief, his return praised for. His return will be that of Ireland's past glory. His memory will comfort in the dreary days, his athletic feats an example to match. And as he rose like the Phoenix, so the dawn already glimmers as he walks his road.

> The silent cock shall crow at last. The west shall shake the east awake.

THE LETTER (pp. 615–619)

This is the last word of ALP before forgetting as we pass on from this sleep. She addresses the king or priest, defending HCE. Her letter jumps from detail to detail, memory to memory, and is in fact written to HCE himself. "Yon clouds will soon disappear looking forwards at a fine day." She describes his adoration of her, the pleasure he gave her, his honesty, his idealism—"that was the prick of the spindle to me that gave me the keys to dreamland."* Then she belittles his detractors "(the lies is coming out on them frecklefully)" and hopes they forget him—or if they continue to doubt his Irishness she wouldn't be surprised by a little violence towards them ("a pipe of twist or a slug of Hibernia metal we could let out" (p. 616)). They would deserve it, the 3 pimps and 2 whores ("Sulvans of Dulkey ... Peris of Monacheena"), and himself the picture of a man and ever adored by salesladies. She would like to see the aforementioned pests brought to justice.

She starts to outline his history. He was fired as a sausage salesman by the prompting of the military. She says they were mistaken. And adds they foisted a bad government into them. Which he stood up to, not afraid of trouble. Then she describes their home. She asks who else could dream himself as 2 sons, "the buck-

---

*Compare page 626: "My lips went livid for from the joy of fear. ... How you said how you'd give me the keys of me heart." It has been thought that kissing, that magical tasting and exchange between human bodies, was unknown to the Celts, whereas the Romans had names for 3 kinds: *osculum* (cheek), *basium* (mouth), *savium* (tongue), all of which are named on page 122. So ALP learns and is grateful. Page 628: "Lps. The keys to. Given!"

et Toolers" (p. 617), or let their "Conan Boyles" knock him into daylight ("Good licks!"). Anyhow, the funeral, Tuesday, "will now shortly occur." Mostly females will be there.

She touches on their treatment by the police, when everyone else shows them such respect, not that she cares ("they can make their beaux to my alce"). She was never chained to a chair, and a widower did not go after her with a fork. So HCE is a gentle civilian while Sully is a drunken thug though a fine bootmaker [bookbinder?], and it would break him to pursue charges.

Now talk is calmer, human, after a few drinks, and it's one woman to one man.

And it's nice, ALP says, to have young ladies ("their demb cheeks" (p. 619)) about (she is referring to their maids), bothering himself, so it doesn't look good, but he is not the one "under the himp of holth" (the hill of Howth) because he is the one who will get up for her.

Signed and P.S.: One of the girls is full up with the places Soldier Rollo is taking her. Their riches are rags to her. But she's kept her self well.

ANNA LIFFEY (pp. 619–628)

The leaf-filled river calls the city to wake, and wants to travel and go for a walk with him before the children are up. She remembers his coming to her father's tailor shop when she was alone. She knows she is old and he is to wake anew and look to the new Liffey lass coming after her. Then she sees the ocean and how small the city is. She too is small again rushing to her father's arms, alone but keeping one leaf still to her of the life behind her, the lips that kissed.

APPENDICES

A Shorter *Finnegans Wake*

DUSK

Tim Finnegan falls down, gets up, goes back to sleep.
H. C. Earwicker is subject to scandalous rumor.
Earwicker flees.
Earwicker evades punishment.
A hen finds a letter from Earwicker's wife.
Pictures from the family album are examined.
The son Shem is a filthy degenerate writer.
Washerwomen talk about the wife, Anna Livia.

EVENING

Shem can't guess the color of his sister's underpants.
Shem draws a map of his mother's bottom.
Earwicker serves the customers and collapses after they leave.
Four old men watch a young couple kiss.

NIGHT

The son Shaun sets out on his mail route.
Shaun admonishes his sister and runs after his hat.
Four old men interrogate Shaun about Earwicker.
A child's cry. Coitus.

DAWN

The Liffey river returns to the ocean.

The Mystery of the Narrator

The narrator, the author's voice, a God, is a singular point of origin yet immanent in every face of her creation, like the dreamer in his dream: The shapes and sensations emerge from some place so hidden from the waking gaze, that its origin seems outside oneself. Memories reshape traumatic and intense experience and all that is persistent, bothersome, and repetitive, the nagging problem, suppressed, forgotten, unfulfilled, neglected, and ignored desires and fears, to create—like the senses calling attention to discomfort and disruption—the image the sleeping eye must see.

You are the narrator of the dreams you read, writer and reader both. In the best art, the writer has become a million readers and every reader the writer in a dream they share. We finish a book like emerging from sleep, a leaf still clinging in our conscience from the rivers of the mind's night thoughts.

The story is in the past. The narration is in the telling and the reading. The future is after the tale is told.

Cycles of Genesis

As is evident in the timeline by A. Walton Litz that is reproduced in Richard Ellman's biography, *Finnegans Wake* might be seen as originally a pair of books: a day book for HCE—an ideal of the sleeper's fallen self, brought low by his children whose battles create the necessity of his return—followed by a night book for Shaun the Post—an ideal of the sleeper's renewed self. By early 1926, these two books were finished, only four years after *Ulysses* was published. It is interesting to consider them thus as a separate work inside the final piece, namely, chapters 2–5 & 7–8 of part I and all of part III.

What is now the first chapter was written later in 1926, an introductory number to establish the "Finnegan's Wake" context. Before that, Joyce had already written a transitional section that is now the middle of the second chapter of part II. Perhaps thinking of the players that this transition section was to use, he inserted another chapter in part I, what is now chapter 6 (usually called "Questions and Answers"; note how smoothly chapter 5 moves to chapter 7 without this intervening chapter). The introduction of the stock characters and elaboration of the Shaun-Shem rivalry indeed provide a valuable set-up for the next part (part II), which uses them much more than the other books do. He might have now seen where (the third chapter of part II) he would use his father's stories of Kersse the Tailor and the Norwegian Captain and of Buckley and the Russian General, something he had long wanted to do.

Through 1927–1929, all of what is now part I, the transitional section, and all of what is now part III were published in *transition*, the Parisian magazine edited by Eugene Jolas. In another few years, chapters 1–3 of part II were finished, elaborating the progressive victories of Shaun over Shem as HCE moves between night and the coming day.

When galleys began to be set in 1937 for the complete work, Joyce still had not written in three of the initial four sketches that he wrote 14 years before. "King Roderick O'Conor" had become the end of the third chapter of part II, and now "The Kiss" was expanded to become the fourth chapter, in which the old remember their youth which is the future leaving them behind. Finally, the last part of the book was written, incorporating the sketches of Saints Kevin and Patrick as the sleeper begins to come back to Ireland.

From 1926, linear and cyclic movements were thus added to the more spatial reflection between parts I and III, i.e., between night and day, between fallen HCE and rising Shaun. The linear movement is described in Structure, *above*. As also described above, the cyclic movement follows the course of nations described by Vico, but with all of the ages present together, i.e., they have a simultaneous origin and end in the mud after the flood.

Each cataclysm seems to be the end of history but only re-forges the same bonds. Perhaps a bond of love might sometime shatter those of piety, shame, and the threat of immortality to allow one to move a little more happily alongside the more vicious circles of history.

A nation arises after piety, modesty, and the sense of an immortal soul give rise to the institutions of religion, marriage, and burial. Piety is perhaps most closely associated with Vico's divine age, modesty with the heroic, and immortality with the popular. When piety—fear of God—wanes, the divine age is no longer the dominant character. When modesty and shame wither, the dominance of the heroic character gives over to the popular. And when the sense of immortality dies, so does the nation with all of its characters, washed away in a new deluge but lingering on into the next cycle. And relived every night by the sleeping mind whence history springs.

The biblical flood came 1656 years after the creation of the world. Famine forced the Semites into Egypt 1656 years after that. Jesus was born 1656 years after that, and 1656 years later Oliver Cromwell ravaged Ireland. 1656 years after the founding of Rome the last effort to re-unite the east and west churches failed (when Rome added *filioque* to the creed).

Finnegans Wake was published 1656 years after the death of Finn Mac Cool. In Viconian Cycle, *above*, I suggested that Finn represented a "divine" age, whose dominance therefore ended in the year 283—we might as well say it lasted 283 years. HCE represents an "heroic" age, ending in 1132, when Diarmaid Mac Murrough sacked Kildare and had the abbess of St. Brighid raped. Cromwell's arrival ended a "popular" age during which the Catholic Normans had readily assimilated. The 283 years following are both the lingering dissipation of the previous age and a divine age at the beginning of a new nation. It is a period of both ending and beginning.

283 years after the biblical flood, Noah died and Abram met Sarai. 283 years after Cromwell, the world was descending through economic disaster into totalitarian war and *Finnegans Wake* was being written—a thunderous creation of a new faith followed by heroic struggles over interpretation.

The Ravisht Bride

1132 A.D. Men like to ants or emmets wondern upon a groot hwide Whallfisk which lay in a Runnel. Blubby wares upat Ublanium.

566 A.D. On Baalfire's night of this year after deluge a crone that hadde a wickered Kish for to hale dead tunes from the bog lookit under the blay of her Kish as she ran for to sothisfeige her cowrieosity and be me sawl but she found hersell sackvulle of swart goody quickenshoon ant small illigant brogues, so rich in sweat. Blurry works at Hurdlesford.

(Silent.)

566 A.D. At this time it fell out that a brazenlockt damsel grieved (*sobralasolas!*) because that Puppette her minion was ravisht of her by the ogre Puropeus Pious. Bloody wars in Ballyaughacleeaghbally.

1132 A.D. Two sons at an hour were born until a goodman and his hag. These sons called themselves Caddy and Primas. Primas was a santryman and drilled all decent people. Caddy went to Winehouse and wrote o peace a farce. Blotty words for Dublin. [pp. 13–14]

Four entries in a chronicle of Dublin, but labelled in a confusing way, as if it moves backwards in time to a mysterious, perhaps sacred, point and then forwards again.* Or, as suggested by the changing names for Dublin, if A.D. stands for *ante diluvium* as well as *anno domini*, the first two entries reflect a time before some destructive event, a flood that changed everything. The second two entries are for a time since. Or rather, because the second entry clearly specifies "after deluge," we see the reflection of such a scheme, the past reflected in the future and *vice versa*. But where is that moment, the opposite of HCE's thunder, not spoken of or otherwise signalled except that it is

(Silent.)

The progression of dates suggests two solutions: Arithmetically, they move to and from 283 (half of 566, a quarter of 1132), the year of Finn Mac Cool's slaying; geometrically, the turning point is 0, or rather the point between two years from which the

---

*Similar hiatuses are found on pages 334 and 501.

calendars are numbered. Alternatively, the years are the same on each side of the turning point, the chroniclers moving back and forth between current events and those in the past.* In this case, the date at the center is in 1132. Indeed, on page 387 Johnny MacDougall recalls "the year of the flood 1132." All 4 old men—in the fourth chapter of the second part of the book, the second-to-last section that Joyce wrote, expanding one of his initial sketches, The Kiss—recall events of that year. Marcus Lyons calls it "the freebutter year of Notre Dame" [p. 388], Lucas Tarpey "the year of buy in disgrace" [p. 391], and Matt Gregory includes the day: "old year's eve 1132" [p. 397].

The riverend Clarence Sterling—who has examined the mysteries and provided most of the discoveries in this appendix, in papers, internet discussion lists, and personal correspondence—explains that old year's eve in Ireland was the evening of January 31, the start of Oimelc (also known as Imbolg), one of the principal Celtic holidays and sacred to Brighid. Over two or three nights and days, people turned from winter's stillness to look towards spring. In Christian times, Brighid became St. Bridget, also commonly called Bride, and February 1 & 2 became, respectively, St. Bridget's feast day and Candlemas, the purification of Mary (as well as James Joyce's birthday). In the liturgical calendar, the nearest Sunday to Candlemas marked the turn from counting days *since* Christmas to counting the days *to* Easter. In 1132, that day was January 31, the only clear date that appears in *Finnegans Wake*: "31 Jan. 1132 A.D." (p. 420). It is the date on the letter written by Shem for his mother and carried by Shaun for his father, the letter revealed in the midden heap by Biddy the Hen, an incarnation of Brighid, and the letter stands for the book itself. Why?

Why? One's apurr apuss a story about brid ... [p. 597]

---

*"In looking at these [12th-century] documents we will be moving back and forth between centuries as the Irish often used sixth- or seventh-century figures or events to illustrate the problems of later centuries." (Mary Condren, *The Serpent and the Goddess: Women, Religion, and Power in Celtic Ireland*, 1989, Harper Collins)

Johnny mentions "Her Grace the bishop Senior" (p. 387) among a trio of powerful women; St. Bridget is said to have been a bishop in Ireland.

> Johnny. ... and after that then there was the official landing of Lady Jales Casemate, in the year of the flood 1132 S.O.S., and the christening of Queen Baltersby, the Fourth Buzzersbee, according to Her Grace the bishop Senior, off the whate shape ... [p. 387]

Marcus's "freebutter year of Notre Dame" refers to Bridget as Mary of the Gaels and to the story that no one went without butter at Kildare, her monastery. Her precursor, the goddess Brighid, was embodied in the cream at the top of the morning's milking. Marcus describes a man and woman in bed together, the woman on top.

> Marcus. ... and then there was the Frankish floot of Noahsdobahs, from Hedalgoland, round about the freebutter year of Notre Dame 1132 P.P.O. or so, disumbunking from under Motham General Bonaboche, (noo poopery!) in his half a grey traditional hat ... [p. 388]

Lucas avoids alluding to Bridget while recalling the year 1132. He describes a lone woman holding on to some power while dressed as a man, but the king's glory eclipses her. He calls the time "the year of buy in disgrace," referring to the difficulty St. Malachy had when named bishop of Ireland in 1132 to enforce the Roman liturgy and end the hereditary succession (yes, father to son) of religious offices—he eventually had to buy the bishop's crook (*see* Magic Numbers, *above*). He may also be referring to bride-price, the gifts given by a man to his bride's family, which practice was replaced by its reverse, the dowry.

There may also be a lingering sense of shame that the Armagh families did sell their rights to Malachy. The phrase is also "*boy in disgrace,*" acknowledging the crimes of those who have forced their will (for example, in 1132, 1169, and 1768). So often expressed as man against woman, this relates to the story about Bridget, as we shall see momentarily.

> Lucas. And, O so well they could remembore at that time, when Carpery of the Goold Fins was in the kingship of Poolland, Mrs Dowager Justice Squalchman, foorsitter, in her fullbottom wig and beard, (Erminia Reginia!) in or aring or around about the year of buy in disgrace 1132 or 1169 or 1768 Y.W.C.A., at the Married Male Familyman's Auctioneer's court in Arrahnacuddle. [pp. 390–391]

And Matt describes an old couple settled in domestic tranquility, away from the troubled past, reading their letters, or studying old manuscripts (the Senchus Mor is the old Celtic body of laws, attributed to Brighid but revised by Patrick), before sleep, on "old year's eve," the day of reflection that we've already discussed.*

> Matt. ... when it so happen they were all sycamore and by the world forgot, ... and read a letter or two every night, before going to dodo sleep atrance, with their catkins coifs, in the twilight, a capitaletter, for further auspices, on their old one page codex book of old year's eve 1132, M.M.L.J. old style, their Senchus Mor, by his fellow girl, the Mrs Shemans, in her summer seal houseonsample ... [p. 397]

So what happened in Bridget's story to make the eve of her day in 1132 so central, around which memories are pained, evasive, and deceiving? The 16th-century "Annals of Loch Cé" includes an entry that resembles the third event chronicled on pages 13–14 ("Puppette her minion was ravisht of her by the ogre Puropeous Pious"):

> The kalends [1st] of January on the 6th feria [Friday], the 10th of the moon [waxing gibbous, half a hat]; the age of the Lord thirty-two years, and a hundred and a thousand [1132]. The abbot's house of Cill-Dara [Kildare] was captured by the Ui-Ceinnselaigh [Hy Kinsella] against the comarb [counselor] of Brighid, and burned, and a large part of the church, and a great many were slain there; and the nun herself was carried off a prisoner, and put into a man's bed.

---

*Coincidentally, James Joyce died on a later "old year's eve," December 31, 1940, in the Julian calendar (corrected to January 13, 1941, in the Gregorian, the one we use today).

As mentioned elsewhere in these pages, it was Diarmaid Mac Murrough who led this especially violent raid that included the rape of the abbess of Kildare, the embodiment of St. Bridget, herself the continuation of the goddess Brighid. His purpose was the destruction of her authority, "Her Grace." The act may or may not be directly related to Malachy's mission to bring the Brighidine Irish church in line with Roman rule. Diarmaid was, however, famed for his generosity to the church, and Dublin was a center of support for Roman dominance. Whatever the larger politics, Diarmaid by this manner became king of Leinster and his own kinswoman became abbess of Kildare.

Thirty-four years later, the last high king of Ireland, Rory O' Conor, took up the cause of a man whose wife was kidnapped by the same Diarmaid Mac Murrough. In exile, Diarmaid sought the help of the Normans, promising his kingship and his daughter to Strongbow, who came and conquered in 1169 (*see* History, *above*). In 1768, the Irish Catholic church added to its service a prayer for the English monarch's health.

> Once Bank of Ireland's. ... Milchbroke. Wrongly spilled. ... Now Bunk of England's. [p. 420]

> Ay, ay. The good go and the wicked is left over. ... Ah, well sure, that's the way. As the holymaid of Kunut said to the haryman of Koombe. ... Woman. Squash. Part. Ay, ay. By decree absolute. [p. 390]

The year 1132 began with the rape of Brighid/Bridget/Bride, the violation of Irish womanhood itself and of a vital continuation of the past. On page 500, the rape is echoed in the betrayal of Parnell, dangers facing Isolde, and the reverend Swift's "sosie sesthers" (p. 3). As the riverend Sterling asserts in more thorough and interesting argument than I have offered here, it is the seminal (the pun is meaningful) event of *Finnegans Wake*, repeated before and since, a brutal Irish church-sanctioned version of "penisolate war" (p. 3), of Nicholas of Cusa's *coincidentia oppositorum*.

> —Slog Slagt and sluaghter! Rape the daughter! ...

—Sold! I am sold! Brinabride! My ersther! My sidster! Brinabride, goodbye! Brinabride! I sold! [p. 500]

Such a kiss has brought together opposites, but it broke a unity around which opposites flowed in a natural circle of being. After such a kiss, there is no return. From St. Bridget's eve of that year, 31 Jan., a very different eve than the previous year's, more like a wake for the old goddess than a feast to welcome and bless the new year, we must look both back to what was and forward to what came to be, good as well as bad, to forgive as well as forget, find love instead of more reason to hate. That is the date of the letter, which stands for the book, which is dreamed in your head where all, the odd moment of respite and grace, between acts, is

(Silent.)